Life on the
Somerset & Dorset Railway

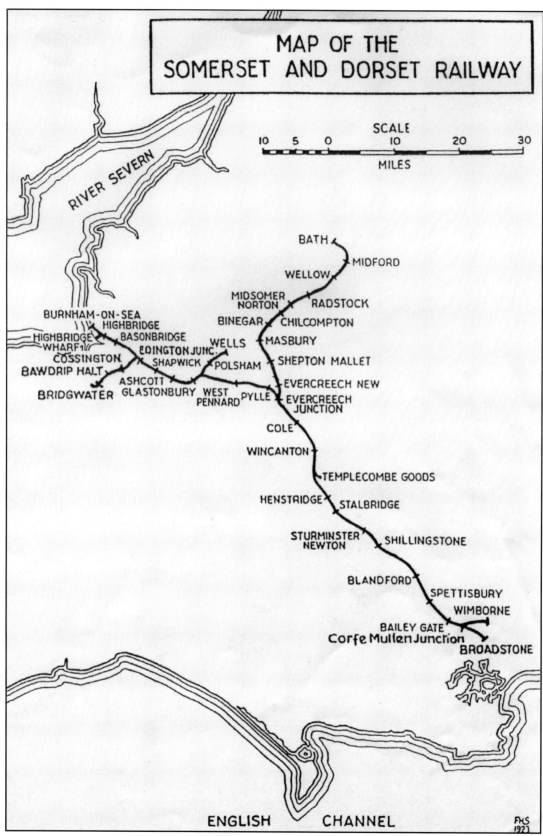

This 1923 map of the Somerset & Dorset Railway shows all stations except the halts of Stourpaine & Durweston, Charlton Marshall, Corfe Mullen, which all opened in 1928, and Shoscombe & Single Hill, which opened in 1929. (*by courtesy of the Somerset & Dorset Railway Trust*)

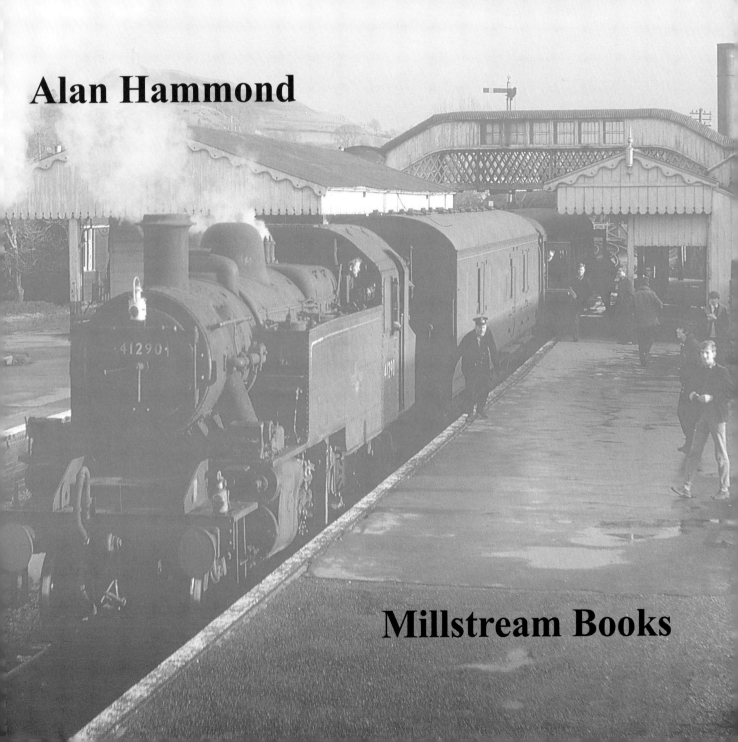

Life on the
Somerset & Dorset Railway

Alan Hammond

Millstream Books

This book is dedicated
to my wife and best friend
Christine
for all the support and enormous help
she has given me over the years with my S&D books

First published in 1999 by
Millstream Books, 18 The Tyning, Bath BA2 6AL

Set in Times New Roman and printed in Great Britain by
The Amadeus Press, Huddersfield, West Yorkshire

© Alan Hammond 1999

ISBN 0 948975 55 5

British Library Cataloguing-in-Publication Data:
a catalogue record for this book is available from the British Library

Foreword

The *Somerset & Dorset Railway* must be one of the most famous and interesting lines in the country, even though it ceased to exist 33 years ago. What is it about this particular railway that has caught the imagination of so many people?

Former staff, passengers, historians, writers and people like myself who have only come to the memory of the S&D in recent years will all enjoy *Life on the Somerset & Dorset Railway*.

I first heard about the S&D in the late 1960s when one day I got into conversation with Arnold Ridley, during a break in filming an episode of *Dads' Army* up in Norfolk. Arnold (better known as Private Godfrey) and I were enjoying the warm sunshine, and the conversation turned to the subject of railways. I asked him how he got the idea for his very famous play *The Ghost Train*. He told me that once, on a journey from Birmingham to his home in Bath, he had a fairly long wait at Mangotsfield, the junction just north of Bristol, and he had started to imagine the plot of the play whilst waiting for his connection. He then asked me if I knew of the Somerset

& Dorset Railway, and I had to admit that I did not. He obviously knew it very well and had a great affection for the line. He enthused about the picturesque landscape, the feeling of being on a community line, run for the convenience of its passengers; if you were a regular traveller, the staff became your friends, one was well looked after, comfortable and safe. One particular station he mentioned which caught my imagination was Evercreech Junction. What a wonderful name.

Some great memories of the age of steam were brought back to us when we filmed an episode for *Dads' Army* on the North Norfolk Railway, entitled *The Royal Train*.

I have always been particularly fond of the counties of Dorset & Somerset and the lovely scenery in the area, and in recent years have made several visits to the West and East Somerset Railways and have cemented many friendships there. Recently I have become more aware of the Somerset & Dorset when I visited Washford (the headquarters of the S&D Railway Trust) to unveil a plaque in the small but delightful rock garden dedicated to the memory of driver Donald Beale. What a splendid day that was.

Two years ago my wife and I were staying at a very nice hotel in Midsomer Norton for a few days holiday and to my surprise the old S&D station was close by. I paid several visits to it and on more than one occasion imagined the train passing through, steam up, whistle blowing. During our stay we also visited Evercreech where I stood on the grass and envisaged all the noise and bustle of that busy Junction in the past. We also visited Shepton Mallet, with its magnificent viaducts, and Radstock, retracing the line there. I look forward to spending more time in this area where I may have the opportunity of finding out more about the S&D.

Alan Hammond paints us a clear picture of those great days, when railway companies and their staff really cared about their passengers and that was certainly true of the Somerset & Dorset. For those who are new to the line, they will, I am sure find immediate interest in the joyful period so lovingly documented in this book with its marvellous photographs and memories.

I am delighted to have been asked to write this foreword and I wish Alan great success with the book.

Bill Pertwee, 1999

Introduction & Acknowledgements

As we enter the new Millennium my thoughts go back to the men and women who worked on the Somerset & Dorset Railway, where generations of railway families made the S&D into one of the most famous lines in Britain.

I have been privileged to meet, record and write the memories of many of these people in my previous three books on the S&D. Over the years I have received many photographs from them, most of which have not been published before. I thought that I should publish these as a lasting tribute to all S&D people. I have also included many pictures taken by well-known photographers. Wherever possible, I have tried to personalize the photographs with the names of the staff. Also in the book is a selection of memories of the S&D from various people who worked or travelled on the line.

You cannot put such a book as this together without plenty of help and encouragement. I would personally like to thank my publisher Tim Graham who has again given me great support; Bill Pertwee, Patron of the Somerset & Dorset Railway Trust, for writing the foreword to my book; and both Andy Moon and Roy Pitman, who have given helpful advice and spent many hours in checking the manuscript. Special thanks are due to all the contributors of stories and photographs in the book, and to Len Barry for producing the prints. Thanks also go to the S&D Trust, Fred, Joan and Andrew Fisher, Joyce Bell, Betty Spiller, Percy Parsons, John Rice, Gordon Hatcher, Maurice and Norah Cook, Keith Barrett, John Sawyer, Frank Staddon, Bob Downes, Norman Cook, Dave Boston and Alan Grieve. As many photographs are from the collections of S&D staff, a reader may well recognise a photograph that he or she took. In this case, I offer my apologies in advance for not being able to credit you in person.

There is always a tinge of sadness when former staff pass away. Recently we have lost Ron Gray, George Skinner, Les Willsher, Eric Elford, Les Cuss, Cyril Beale, Norman White, Trevor Sprague and Donald Beale.

I hope you enjoy *Life on the Somerset & Dorset Railway*; let's hope the memory of the S&D will live on well into the next century and even further.

Alan Hammond, Minehead, 1999.

Staff at Templecombe Lower in 1910. The man standing in front of the S&D timetable is Henry John Ware, father of Bernard who was a guard at Bath Green Park. (*Bernard Ware collection*)

Dave Boston – Signalman

In the 1960s I worked as a signalman on the S&D. My favourite box was Bath Junction, it was like a second home to me. The kettle was always on the boil as you never knew who was going to pop in.

I remember a ganger, Albert Reardon. He used to come up the track from Midford on his motorized trolley. It could also tow a trailer for carrying the permanent way gang. Some of the gang I recall were Ces Marsh, Chris Burdon, Ted Elkins and Edgar Parks. Albert would park opposite the box in a little spur and come up for a chat and a can of tea. On his return journey to Midford he used to let me drive the trolley out of the sidings and he would work the points. Albert could make it back to Midford in 15 minutes. Often he would be in front of the Down *Pines*, once or twice the *Pines* nearly catching him up.

There was always something happening, with plenty of locos to see, from 9F's to 2Ps.

On nights Alan Larcombe, who was a porter at Bath Green Park, would drive up on his scooter bringing our supper with him – I remember it well – fish, faggots and nine penn'orth of chips, lovely.

When I was on the 2.00-10.00 shift and it was a bit slow I used to rush out of the box and run down to Lower Bristol Road to have my hair cut at Frank Bealing's and be back in the box within a few minutes. The signalbox toilet was something else, it was ancient and similar to an Elsan type toilet. It was set in a wooden cabinet and very high off the ground; if you were sitting there reading your newspaper your legs could not touch the floor, it was the most odd feeling.

One of my fellow signalman had an allotment by the railway track. He used to charge his wife for the vegetables that he grew. He said it was cheaper for her to buy them off of him than go to the shops.

I recall one busy Whit Monday. I was on early turn 6.00-2.00 when the box to box phone rang. My mate down the line was in a state of panic, he had a coal wagon off the road on the main line and did not have a clue what to do. I told him to put the phone down, sit tight and leave it to me. I got onto control and arranged for the breakdown gang to come out and get the wagon back on the road. Just as the breakdown train arrived at my box, Paul Pearman who was the assistant Superintendent (previously he was the stationmaster at Bath Green Park) arrived at the same time. I explained to him what had happened and although he was wearing a nice suit he jumped on the footplate of the breakdown train and went off with them. Within a short period of time the wagon was righted and things were back to normal. If this happened today it would take hours and cause great chaos and delay.

On another occasion I had a local train off the S&D line. I pulled off my signals and also pulled out the catcher for the tablet. When the train came past the box, somehow the fireman had not lined up the tablet pouch. The metal ring on the pouch only struck the catcher which caused the pouch to fall straight under the wheels of the coaches. It could not fall between the rails because of the wooden crossing so every wheel of the coaches went over it. When I picked it up, the leather pouch which was well padded, was ripped and torn. I thought that's it, pilot working now, the tablet can't go back into the machine. Much to my surprise when I got the tablet out of the wrecked pouch it was still in one piece; I tried to get it into the machine but it would not go, so I got some emery cloth and rubbed it down until it fitted, so that saved the day.

At another signalbox that I worked at we had rats running around the back of the box. They lived in the pit of ashes from our coal stove. I thought it was about time I did something about it so I got three old detonators, wrapped them in cotton waste and then soaked them with paraffin. I took them out to the pile of ashes and shoved them down the holes that the rats had made and then set fire to them. I quickly got back into the box to await the bang but nothing happened. After a while I forgot about it; 30 minutes later there was an enormous loud explosion. I jumped out of my skin; realizing what it was I ran to the back of the box and looked out. There were two more loud bangs which sent the ashes flying everywhere. I did not see another rat for about six months.

I wish I could turn the clock back to my days as an S&D signalman, it was a wonderful and happy time for me and my S&D mates Ron Moore, George Smart, Frank Mann, Reg Staddon, Jack Lake and Jack Frapwell.

The LMS and S&D Home Guard Company photographed at Bath Green Park in June 1943. The personnel, so far as th
(back row) unknown, Dennis Clem (D), Edward Tucker (D), Ern Buffrey (PF), Ron Bean (PC), Walter Weston (P(
(second row) Robert Clothier (SR), Charles Brown (D), Fred Meader (PF), Fred Brooks (D), Robert King (P(
    Dennis Emery (PC), George Adams (SF), Percy Hurd (Loco Department Clerk), unknown
(third row) Thomas Hilton (Water Softener Plant Attendant), Len West (F), Stan Hayward (Carriage & Wagon Examine
    Albert Chapman (Fr), unknown, Robert Ford (F), Ralph Hooper (D)
(fourth row) George Stott (GG), Sidney Maslen (F), unknown (Goods Office Clerk), Harold Barber (D), Norman Rosenburg (I
    William Tosseano (D), Robert Ford (F), Charles Herbert (PC)
(front row) William Mantle (PF), John Barber (PC), Norman White (S), Thomas Every (BW), Tom Gunning (PI
Grades: D =Driver, F=Fireman, PF= Passed Fireman, PC=Passed Cleaner, Fr=Fitter, SF=Senior Fitter, FM=Fitter's Ma

known, with their grades at the time, are as follows, from left to right:

y Pearce (D), Albert Fishlock (GS), Henry Waldron (F), Fred Epps (F), George Coles (F), Edward Bullock (FM)

liam Lee (D), Herbert Hulance (PC), Bill Williams (S), Doug Holden (F), William Wiles (S), Ronald Shearn (PC),

rdon King (PC), Archie Gunning (PF), Lou Adams (Fr), Capt. Fred Jefferies (D), Arthur Tidball (D), Albert Reed (D),

hur King (D), Lt. Reg Iley (Fr), Lt. Ernie Cross (SR), Charlie Crocker (D), Arthur Rowett (S), Bob Cannings (S),

orge Quinn (Control Office, Bath Green Park), Ken Hartley (PC), Ken Norris (PC)

=Goods Shunter, GG=Goods Guard, BB=Bar Boy, S=Signalman, SR=Steam Raiser   (*photograph John Stamp*)

The crew of No.39 pose proudly for the photographer. This locomotive was built in 1879 by Vulcan Foundry and withdrawn from service 46 years later, in 1925. (*Keith Barrett collection*)

A busy scene at Bath Green Park with two BR Standard class 4s, tank engine No.80146, on the left, and tender engine No.75072, both blowing off plenty of steam as the two men on the platform have noticed. (*David Walden*)

The driver surveys his engine, a 4-4-0 No.77, at Bath Green Park – note the bonded warehouse, used by HM Customs and Excise as a store and office. The photograph was taken before 1930. (*Keith Barrett collection*)

BR Standard class 3 No.82041 passes Bath goods yard with the 6.05pm local passenger train stopping at all stations to Binegar, 25th March 1964. (*Martyn Burch*)

A stunning shot of BR Standard class 5 No.73052 with the 4.20pm coming out of Bath on its way to Bournemouth on 19th August 1963. (*Martyn Burch*)

The southbound *Pines Express*, hauled by 2P No.40634 and BR Standard No.73047, passes Bath goods yard, with a Jinty on the next track. The end of a wooden-bodied wagon can be seen on the extreme right. (*Martyn Burch*)

Driver Vic Ball, left, and his fireman Albert Parsons on a wet day at Green Park in 1965 with LMS Stanier 8F No.48706. (*S&DRT collection*)

(*above*) Fireman Cliff Smith stands beside 2P No.40505 in early BR livery at Bath Green Park, c.1948. (*Cliff Smith collection*)

(*right*) Driver Ron Gray, who started work on the S&D at Bath Green Park on 14th July 1934, photographed here in the 1950s. He spent 51 years on the railway – 32 of them on the S&D. Behind him is BR Standard No.82041. (*Ron Gray collection*)

In August 1959 an SR West Country class locomotive accidentally hit a wagon with such force that it subsequently hit a 7F which was out of steam and the latter smashed into the foreman cleaner's office at the end of No.3 Road at Bath Green Park shed. Fortunately nobody was hurt. (*John Stamp*)

Jinty No.47557 pauses briefly from shunting at Green Park on 31st January 1961. 7F No.53805 stands nearby with a 4F in the distance preparing to bank a freight train. (*Martyn Burch*)

BR Standard No.75027 (now preserved) stands in the snow at Green Park on 13th February 1960. (*Martyn Burch*)

Bulleid Pacifics Nos. 34006 *Bude* and 34057 *Biggin Hill* being prepared at Green Park to take out one of the last specials on the S&D, a Locomotive Club of Great Britain Rail Tour on 5th March 1966. (*Martyn Burch*)

Driver Archie Gunning makes last minute checks on pilot engine 8F No.48706 at Bath Green Park before departing south with a Stephenson Locomotive Society special on 6th March 1966. His brother Bill was the driver on the train engine, BR Standard No.80043. (*Keith Barrett Collection*)

Collett 0-6-0 No. 2229 stands in the Green Park approaches on a crisp November day in 1960. It is coupled to what appears to be an engineer's wagon loaded with plant. (*Martyn Burch*)

BR Standard No.75072 arrives at Bath with the 12.00 noon stopping train from Templecombe. Leaning out of his cab is fireman Ray Stokes. (*Keith Barrett collection*)

(*left*) BR Standard No.75073 and Black Five No.44804 haul a train past Bellotts Road on 7th July 1962, soon to pass over bridge No.3 across the Great Western main line and start the long climb to Combe Down Tunnel.

(*below*) BR Standard No.73050 at the same location in the atrocious conditions of 1963. The Ford Prefect seems tiny beside the train. (*both photos Martyn Burch*) (*right*) The southbound *Pines*, hauled by 2P No. 40569 and BR Standard No.73019, working hard up the bank immediately before Claude Avenue Bridge on 13th May 1961.

(*below*) BR Standard No.73052 has just passed Claude Avenue Bridge and climbs on up towards Devonshire Tunnel. Note the WR syphon van behind the locomotive. (*both photos Martyn Burch*)

(*left*) 7F No.53801 steaming well and pulling hard through the snow on the approach to Devonshire Tunnel on 30th January 1954. (*R.E.Toop*)

(*below*) A Home Counties Railway Society Tour train emerges from Devonshire Tunnel and runs down the bank towards Bath on 7th June 1964. The driver on 7F No.53807 was Alwyn Hannam with fireman Don Garrett and on the 4F No.44558 was Fred Fisher with fireman Bruce Briant. (*Martyn Burch*)

4F No.44146 banking a southbound freight train between Devonshire and Combe Down Tunnels on 13th November 1954. The train engine is 7F No.53803. (*R.E.Toop*)

BR Standard No.75071 emerges from Combe Down Tunnel into a very snowy scene in the bitter winter of 1963. (*Martyn Burch*)

BR Standard No.73052 with a train of six coaches has just passed over Tucking Mill Viaduct and is about to enter Combe Down Tunnel in January 1963. (*Martyn Burch*)

(*left and below*) A Jinty 0-6-0 tank with a short train of three wagons of coal and guards van about to enter the southern end of Combe Down Tunnel in January 1963. (*both photos Martyn Burch*)

A lone 8F battles through after a heavy fall of snow at Tucking Mill in January 1963. Who would want to be on the footplate in these conditions? (*Martyn Burch*)

(*above*) In contrast to the previous page, this sylvan scene near Midford shows pilot engine 2P No.40700 and BR Standard No.73052 running easily down the gradient towards the station. (*R.C.Riley*)

(*right*) A view looking south at Midford with the tall backing signal on the platform and the signalbox just in front of the viaduct, July 1964. (*David Walden*)

John Sawyer – Fireman

As a young fireman at Bath Green Park I fired on a few specials. One was the LCGB Wessex Downsman on 2nd May 1965 with 8F No.48309. We really struggled out of Bath and I couldn't understand why; then I realized I'd left the tender handbrake on.

One special I recall well was on Bank Holiday Monday, 30th August 1965. I arrived for work on my bike at about 7.40am. I recall seeing a Standard class 5 loco standing in the boat road blowing a full head of steam with a clean looking footplate but rather a dirty look everywhere else. The front number plate was missing, the number was there but painted on. I thought, well maybe this is our engine for the day. As I booked on I knew the driver was my regular mate Ben Ford. I walked to the engine board and sure enough 73001 was assigned to the special. I made my way to the messroom where Ben was already brewing his tea. I also filled my can (no tea bags in 1965); we had a quick mug each, a railwayman can't start the day without the important things of life. Thinking of that messroom today I can still see the faces of my S&D colleagues Ron Gray, Harry Shearn, Archie Gunning, Bill Rawles, Ian Bunnett, Clive Cater and Dave Norman. The cigarette smoke, the atmosphere, the laughter, the comradeship, they have now disappeared for ever.

Leaving the messroom for the short walk to the loco I was a little nervous. On climbing aboard I noticed we had plenty of steam and water and the fire looked in good condition, at least we were off to a good start. Ben and I did the usual checks before moving off. I looked up at the sky and said to myself "I'm going to need a little help here today". As we moved off shed I proceeded to push the fire forward a little to reveal an evenly burning mass. On arrival at Bath Green Park station our train was almost up to the river bridge; I thought that it looked longer than anything I had fired on before, I would certainly be sweating today. The shunter coupled us up and I was busy with the fire and the injectors to try and give us the best start possible ready for the 1 in 50 climb out of Bath. As I was concentrating on the job in hand our guard Ron Smith came up to the footplate with sweat pouring from his bright red face and said "Morning" I answered "Yeh, 'tis innit". He said the same to Ben and got a slightly different answer, just a plain "is it?"; a bit of a joke between the three of us, this was our usual greeting each time we were put together as a team. Ron said to Ben, "we have 8 coaches on, just under 400 tons and no assistance". In the next breath he uttered "do you think the lad can manage it, Ben?" "Of course", Ben replied.

The Wessex Downsman at Midford on 2nd May 1965. Ben Ford is the driver on 8F No.48309 and John Sawyer his fireman. (*Tom Cox collection*)

Actually the trip went well out of Bath and over the Mendips. We stopped at various places for water and signals and each time we stopped there were many enthusiasts with their cameras. We arrived at Bournemouth Central at 10.45am, took the engine to shed and made our way to the messroom for a bite to eat and an hour's rest. In the messroom all I could hear was these cockney voices; we were told they had worked their way down from Waterloo, so really we were the strangers not them. Ben and I decided to walk down to the beach and spent most of the day there; we had a couple of pints and I thought to myself, my mates back home will never believe me that I was on the beach having a pint and getting paid for it. We worked the same train back in the evening, leaving Bournemouth Central at 20.15. Unfortunately the journey back was not so good and we had trouble almost all of the way. It was not a very good fire which resulted in low steam pressure and low water level. On reaching Shillingstone station again there were lots of people taking photographs. As we approached Evercreech Junction we were about 10 minutes down and things did not look good for the climb over the Mendips. Ben did not seem all that worried, in fact he said "we will have a few minutes longer at Evercreech, John, to give ourselves a chance". The journey seemed to be getting worse but finally we made it

to Masbury and regained some kind of rhythm before reaching Radstock. Of course the next obstacle was to take the single line pouch at Midford. Our engine did not have the Whitaker apparatus fitted to it, so it meant taking the pouch by hand, going at 50 to 60 miles per hour in the dark with just the signalbox lamps for light, then leaning out of the side of the cab, hanging onto the hand-rail with one hand. I then lunged my other arm through the large ring attached to the pouch which was a bit hair raising; fortunately I took the tablet well from Percy Savage. We continued our journey through the Midford valley. (Midford was a favourite place of mine, I used to throw away my yearly issue of a BR railway cap there. I amongst others did not like the caps so the embankment near to Midford station was as good a place as any to dispose of them; there must be quite a few buried there.) We arrived at Bath Green Park only 20 minutes late; it was a pretty tiring day. The next day was a rest day, again I was with Ben and he mentioned in the messroom it was no wonder I had struggled on that return journey as the firebox was covered in clinker. Even though it had been a struggle I thoroughly enjoyed that special. Unfortunately seven months later the line closed, so I was very pleased to know that I had fired on a holiday special on the S&D.

4F No.44559 accelerates away from Midford towards Wellow in the late fifties. Note the Southern three-coach set No.394. The up siding is evidently still in use and a Ford 100E car is parked in the foreground. (*R.E.Toop*)

A classic shot at Midford as BR Standard No.80043 departs south with the 3.20pm train from Bath to Templecombe.   *(R.E.Toop)*

The northbound *Pines Express* at Wellow on 6th July 1959, hauled by 2P No.40652 and BR Standard No.73087, passes 7F No.53807 which has set back into the sidings. There seems to be quite a discussion going on between the 7F crew and possibly two members of the permanent way gang. (*R.C.Riley*)

Fireman Keith Barrett takes it easy on the up *Pines* on pilot engine BR Standard No.75009 with an unidentified 9F as it makes its way through Wellow. (*Keith Barrett collection*)

The tranquil setting of Wellow station in 1963. On the right is the combined building of the stationmaster's office, booking hall and waiting room. Further up on the right there are two wagons in the goods yard. (*Colin Caddy*)

7F No.53804 passing Writhlington signalbox with a northbound train on 2nd August 1958. This box had 19 levers and block instruments to govern the up and down main line and sidings. Signalmen and women who pulled the levers over the years here included Kath Parker, Bernard Ware and Bill Beeho. (*R.E.Toop*)

Radstock North signalbox, photographed on 28th March 1965, had 32 levers. Latterly the wooden box was painted in WR chocolate and cream. Manning the box on summer Saturdays was a nightmare as successive holiday specials could keep the crossing gates closed for long periods. Last to work the box was the well-known Les Willsher. (*Colin Caddy*)

LMS class 3F No.47276 busy shunting wagons at Norton Hill Colliery. (*Keith Barrett collection*)

Station staff at Midsomer Norton a century ago. The stationmaster stands on the left-hand side. (*Will Locke collection*)

Midsomer Norton on a winter Sunday – the signals are off, nobody is around and the gardens have been dug ready for spring planting. The Thornycroft Nippy van in the yard provides a little bit of GWR intrusion. All told, a splendid scene which may one day be re-created. (*Eric Rimmer*)

(*right*) Porter/signalman Stan Jones stands proudly on the platform of Midsomer Norton station in 1948. (*Helen Edwards collection*)

(*below*) The signalbox at Midsomer Norton, seen here in 1962, was probably one of the most photographed boxes on the S&D. In the 1900s it was covered in roses and staff would sell them in aid of the local hospital. Joe Crouchen had the sad task of pulling the last lever. (*Eric Rimmer*)

BR Standard No.75002 at Midsomer Norton south in the 1960s. The driver is looking back for the guard's flag before restarting the journey south. (*Eric Rimmer*)

Nearing Midsomer Norton is BR Standard No.73051 with an unknown rebuilt West Country. (*Eric Rimmer*)

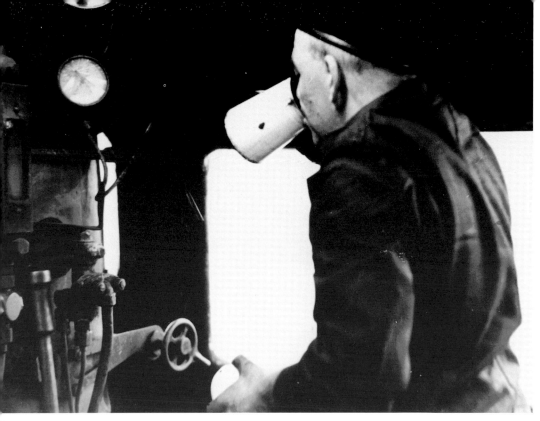

(*left*) Fireman Cliff Smith enjoying a can of tea on BR Standard No.73052 near Chilcompton on 13th August 1961 (*Cliff Smith collection*)

(*below*) A rather dirty BR Standard No.76026 on an up train near Midsomer Norton – a sad occasion for everyone as this photograph was taken on the last day of service. (*David Walden*)

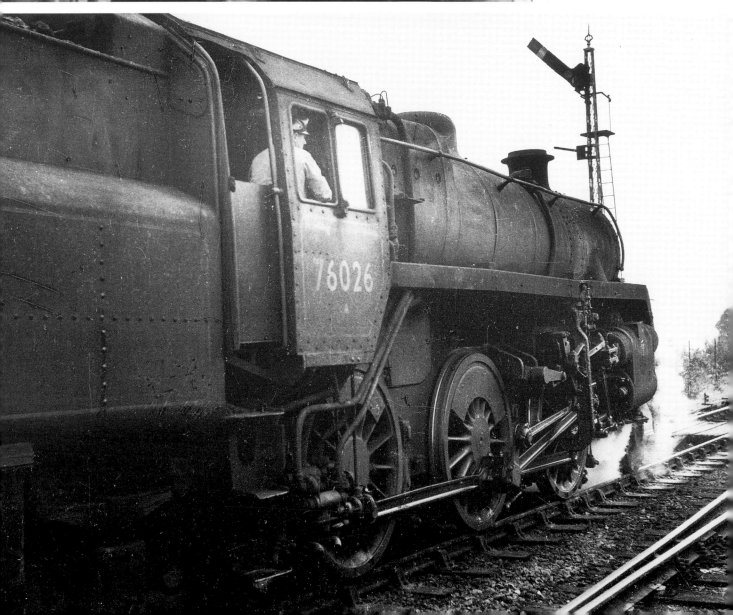

Two shots of BR Standard class 5s, taken on 26th January 1963 during that winter's prolonged arctic conditions: (*above*) No.73047 leaves the short Chilcompton Tunnel with the 1.10pm Bath to Templecombe local train while (*below*) No.73021 passes Chilcompton station, also with an up local passenger train. (*both photos R.E.Toop*)

EACH WEEKDAY
To LONDON (Waterloo)

FROM	DEPART	RETURN FARES SECOND CLASS	ARRIVAL ON RETURN
	a.m.	s. d.	p.m.
RADSTOCK NORTH	7a 18	34/0	9a 59
MIDSOMER NORTON SOUTH ...	7a 29	33/6	9a 53
BINEGAR	7a 45	32/0	B
SHEPTON MALLET (Charlton Rd.)	7a 58	31/0	9a 32
EVERCREECH NEW ...	8a 3	30/0	9a 20
HIGHBRIDGE for Burnham-on-Sea	7b 0	36/6	10b 12
GLASTONBURY & STREET ...	7b 30	33/0	9b 46
WEST PENNARD	7b 40	31/6	9b 35
EVERCREECH JUNCTION ...	8a 14	30/0	9a 13
COLE	8a 20	29/0	9a 6
WINCANTON	8a 30	28/0	8a 56
WATERLOO ... ... arr.	11 8	—	—

Return from
WATERLOO ... ... dep. 6-0 p.m. the Same Day.

a—Change at Templecombe in each direction.
b—Change at Evercreech Junction and Templecombe in each direction.
B—Stops to set down. Guard to be informed by passengers wishing to alight.

EACH WEEKDAY
POOLE & BOURNEMOUTH WEST

FROM	DEPART		RETURN FARES SECOND CLASS	
			To Poole	To Bournemouth
	a.m.	a.m.	s. d.	s. d.
BATH (Green Park)	6 48	9 53	12/9	13/9
MIDFORD	6 59	—	12/0	13/0
WELLOW	7 5	—	11/6	12/6
RADSTOCK NORTH	7 18	10 17	10/6	11/6
MIDSOMER NORTON SOUTH ...	7 29	10 27	10/6	11/3
CHILCOMPTON	7 37	10 36	10/3	10/9
BINEGAR	7 45	—	10/0	10/6
SHEPTON MALLET (Charlton Rd.)	7 58	10 53	9/6	10/0
HIGHBRIDGE for BURNHAM -on-SEA	7a 0	9a 45	11/9	12/9
BASON BRIDGE	7a 4	9a 49	11/6	12/6
EDINGTON BURTLE	7a 12	9a 57	10/9	11/9
SHAPWICK	7a 18	10a 3	10/6	11/3
ASHCOTT	7a 23	10a 8	10/6	11/0
GLASTONBURY & STREET ...	7a 30	10a 17	10/0	10/6
WEST PENNARD	7a 40	10a 28	9/0	9/6
PYLLE HALT	7a 50	10a 38	9/0	9/6
EVERCREECH NEW	8 3	10 59	9/0	9/6
EVERCREECH JUNCTION ...	8 14	11 5	9/0	9/6
COLE	8 20	10b 53	8/6	9/0
WINCANTON	8 30	11 16	8/0	8/6
	a.m.	p.m.		
POOLE ... ... arr.	10 26	12 43		
BOURNEMOUTH WEST ... arr.	10 45	12 55		

Return the Same Day by any train affording a service through to destination.
a—Change at Evercreech Junction.   b—Change at Wincanton.

SPECIMEN DAY FARES

Available By Any Train Weekdays and Sundays (where train service permits) for return by any train the same day affording a service through to destination.

For full details see separate pamphlet.

(Where First Class accommodation is available, First Class tickets are issued at approximately 50% above the Second Class Fare).

	Return Fares Second Class s. d.			Return Fares Second Class s. d.
From BATH (Green Park)		**From MIDFORD**		
To Bitton ...	2 0	To Bath (Green Park)	1 6	
Bristol T.M.	3 0			
Cheltenham Spa ...	11 0			
Cole ...	7 6	**From MIDSOMER NORTON**		
Evercreech Junction ...	6 9	**SOUTH**		
Gloucester	10 0	To Bath (Green Park)	3 3	
Mangotsfield ...	2 9	Shepton Mallet (C. Rd.) ...	3 3	
Midsomer Norton South ...	3 3			
Radstock North ...	2 9			
Warmley ...	2 6			
Weston-Super-Mare ...	8 0	**From RADSTOCK NORTH**		
		To Bath (Green Park)	2 9	
		Shepton Mallet (C. Rd.) ...	3 6	
From CHILCOMPTON				
To Bath (Green Park)	3 9			
Shepton Mallet (C. Rd.) ...	2 9			
		From SHEPTON MALLET		
		(Charlton Road)		
		To Bath (Green Park)	5 6	
From COLE		Wincanton	3 6	
To Bath (Green Park) ...	7 6			
Shepton Mallet (C. Rd.) ...	2 9			
Wincanton	1 9			
		From WELLOW		
		To Bath (Green Park)	2 0	
From EVERCREECH JUNC.				
To Bath (Green Park) ...	6 9			
Glastonbury and Street ...	2 9			
Shepton Mallet (C. Rd.) ...	1 9	**From WINCANTON**		
Wincanton	2 9	To Bath (Green Park)	8 6	
		Salisbury ...	8 0	
		Shepton Mallet (C. Rd.) ...	3 6	
From EVERCREECH NEW		Sherborne	3 0	
To Bath (Green Park)	6 3	Sturminster Newton ...	3 3	
Glastonbury and Street ...	3 0	Yeovil	3 6	
Wincanton	3 0			

NOTE — The above fares are liable to alteration.

Children under Three years of age, Free, Three and under Fourteen years of age, Half-fare. (Fractions of a penny reckoned as one penny)

Tickets can be obtained in advance at Booking Stations and Agencies.

Further information will be supplied on application to Stations, Agencies or to Mr. H. BASTIN. District Superintendent. Temple Meads Station. Bristol 1 (Telephone 2-1001 Extension 208 or 214), or to Mr. D. S. HART, Divisional Manager, Transom House, Victoria Street, Bristol, (Tel. 21001; Ext. 663.)

Paddington Station, W.2.
August, 1962.

Printed by THE SOMER PRESS Ltd., Church Square, Midsomer Norton.   B7/486

(*above*) Moorewood Sidings 19-lever signalbox was the last built on the S&D, in 1914. Traffic was mainly stone from Emborough Quarry. Ernie Cross was the last to work this box which closed in 1965. (*Keith Barrett collection*)
(*below*) Pilot engine 4F No.44560 working hard with an unknown 7F near Binegar. With the amount of smoke coming from the chimney of the 4F, she is probably burning north country coal. (*Dorothy Down collection*)

(*above*) The signalman gazes happily out of the window of Binegar signalbox on a spring day in 1965. This box was in constant use when traffic was banked up Masbury Summit as it controlled the security of the engine coming back wrong line to Binegar. Signalman Michael Reakes pulled the last lever here. (*Colin Caddy*)

(*right*) Fred Uphill, who started as a porter at Binegar on 28th May 1937. Note his Somerset Joint Company cap badge. (*Fred Uphill collection*)

A marvellous shot of a Black Five No.44917 piloted by 4F No.44523 passing through Binegar station with a northbound passenger train for Manchester. (*R.E.Toop*)

Binegar station on 2nd May 1965. This being a Sunday, both up and down signals are pulled off. Everything is in tidy order, with fire buckets hung on the wall, Whitaker's banking engine key apparatus prominent and not a soul around. (*Keith Barrett collection*)

2P No.40564 and Battle of Britain class No.34110, *66 Squadron,* with the southbound *Pines Express* passing Binegar signalbox on 13th July 1957. (*R.E.Toop*)

A spring scene at Binegar as BR Standard No.80043 arrives with the 3.35pm Bristol to Bournemouth train. The tall man on the right is stationmaster Norman Down talking to one of the porters. His lovely wife Dorothy often made cups of tea for waiting photographers. (*Keith Barrett collection*)

7F No.53806 working hard as it passes Masbury station with a northbound passenger train comprising nine corridor coaches. (*R.E.Toop*)

Masbury station looking south on 19th May 1965. In the Second World War, the Americans used this halt extensively to service their nearby camp. For such a small station it had some fine railway buildings including the stationmaster's house which is still occupied by former S&D relief stationmaster, Wilfred Couling. (*Colin Caddy*)

The sad sight of Winsor Hill signalbox, the only box on the S&D built completely of stone. It closed in 1948 after many years protecting the tunnels and sidings of Hamwood and Winsor Hill Quarry. The signalmen in its heyday were Harry Button and Harry Hovey. (*Colin Caddy*)

Snow scenes on the S&D: (*left, above*) 7F No.53803 is making hard work with the 12.35pm goods as it approaches Winsor Hill Tunnel in January 1955 – the signalbox is just visible on the right-hand side. (*left, below*) Jinty No.47557 is stuck with her snow plough trapped in a 10-foot drift north of Winsor Hill on 7th January 1963. 19 members of the track gang finally dug her out many hours later. (*above*) Two BR Standards and a Jinty snowbound near Masbury summit in an abortive attempt to free the down mail from Bath, January 1963. (*below*) The 1963 winter was the worst on record as this picture shows with the trackbed completely covered. Nothing moved for three days along this stretch near Winsor Hill. Many cans of tea were brewed in the permanent way hut as gangs worked to shift the snow in these arctic conditions. (*photo above Bill Silk collection, other photos John Stamp*)

(*above*) Driver Steve Collins enjoying his pipe on the footplate of an 8F while climbing towards Shepton Mallet in the fifties. (*Steve Collins collection*)

(*left*) A smiling Emily Poole with her trusty bike outside the parcels office at Shepton Mallet where she worked in the 1940s. (*Emily Poole collection*)

Shepton Mallet Charlton Road signalbox bordered by a fine array of flowers and shrubs. It had 26 levers and was situated in the middle of the down platform. Ted Lambert was the signalman for a number of years. Note the Ford Zephyr and the permanent way motorized trolley in the bay. (*Eric Rimmer*)

Another shot of the Wessex Downsman on 2nd May 1965 (see page 28). The unassisted 8F No.48309 stops for water, photographs and admiration at Shepton Mallet before heading on for Bournemouth. (*David Walden*)

Part of the attraction of the S&D was the scenic nature of the line. This is amply illustrated in this photograph of BR Standard No.73052 heading southbound over Charlton Road Viaduct and into Shepton Mallet station in July 1964. (*David Walden*)

(*above*) In October 1956 a film was made by British Rail on emergency single line working, using Binegar and Shepton Mallet stations which were called Boiland and Averton Hammer for the film. This photograph shows driver Jack Hix and fireman Gordon Hatcher at Shepton Mallet on BR Standard No.75071, receiving instructions from the film unit. (*Ivo Peters, courtesy of Julian Peters*)

(*right*) The Gunning brothers, Archie and Bill, with 8F No. 48706 and BR Standard No. 80043 heading a special to Bournemouth on the last day of service. It is seen approaching Shepton Mallet station having just crossed Charlton Road Viaduct. (*Keith Barrett collection*)

(*above*) Evercreech New with 9F No.92245 passing through with a northbound passenger train. The array of warning notices on both sides of the crossing at the end of the platform was quite amazing. (*Keith Barrett collection*)

(*below*) Evercreech New signalbox on the down platform next to a kiln belonging to Evercreech Lime & Stone Company, photographed on 2nd March 1956. It was an attractive box with 20 levers and a block switch. James Gould was the well-known signalman here in the 1940s. (*R.M.Casserley*)

Southern and London Midland & Scottish Railway Companies.
(hereinafter called the Company)
SOMERSET AND DORSET RAILWAY JOINT COMMITTEE.

(4/47)

43635

Stock.
(S. & D. 253)
8-45.

CONSIGNMENT NOTE AND WAYBILL for Live Stock (other than Wild Animals) to be carried by Passenger Train or other similar service.

Date 14 August 1957

From EVERCREECH NEW Station to GILLINGHAM Station Co.

Via GILLINGHAM T/COMBE Train 5.47 PM

Full Name and Address of Sender MR K. MOGER WESTCOMBE

Full Name and Address of Consignee REDLANDS POULTRY FARM, GILLINGHAM

Owning Company, No., and Description of Vehicle

No.	Description of Live Stock.	Brands or Marks (overseas traffic when not charged by weight).	Weight. Lbs.	Rate. s.	Rate. d.	Paid on. s.	Paid on. d.	To Pay. £	To Pay. s.	To Pay. d.	Paid. £	Paid. s.	Paid. d.
1	Box Pidgeons		2	1	8								
								OPEN STAMP. DL 97988					

Declared value ... ... £
Percentage on excess value £

TOTAL £ 1 8

Evercreech Junction looking north from under the footbridge on 2nd March 1956. Note the advertisement board on the wall of the waiting room depicting one of the Brylcreem boys. (*R.M.Casserley*)

Ivatt tank No.41296 about to shunt two trucks into the sidings after taking on water at Evercreech Junction in 1965. This engine worked until the end of the S&D and was scrapped in July 1966. (*David Walden*)

Five Evercreech Junction porters: (*below left*) Betty Simms, seen here in 1942, was the first lady porter employed at the station, in 1940. She was joined by Betty Spiller and Joyce Reakes, and they were known up and down the line as 'the firm'. (*Betty Cox, née Simms, collection*) (*above left*) Betty Spiller, née Lambert, at her wedding in 1945 to Templecombe fireman Ron Spiller. The happy couple are seated on an S&D dray, used in the goods yard at Evercreech. Note the letters S&DJ on the side of the dray. (*Betty Spiller collection*) (*right*) the third member of 'the firm' at Evercreech, Joyce Reakes. (*Betty Spiller collection*) (*below*) Vic Freak and David Kerle pose happily in the station gardens at Evercreech in the 1950s. (*Vic Freak collection*)

(*above*) The last day at Evercreech Junction, 5th March 1966, shows four proud railwaymen to the end – from left to right, stationmaster Alec Stowe, Charlie Vaughan, Eddie Riggs and Vic Freak. (*Vic Freak collection*)

(*left*) A happy group of porters at Evercreech Junction – from left to right, Frank Padfield, Gerald Griggs and Eddie Riggs in the 1950s (*Vic Freak collection*)

(*right*) Fireman Cyril May, left, and driver Cecil Cooper in the cab of a 3F in Evercreech North sidings in 1947. The engine looks in a sorry state – the number could do with a lick of paint. (*Fred Parsons*)

Frank Staddon – Guard

I spent most of my working life on the S&D as a porter and guard. My workmates were a great bunch to work with – all types of characters with a story to tell or a joke to play. Sitting back in my comfortable armchair with my S&D photographs around me, the stories flood back.

I was a young porter in the 1940s at Bath Green Park station. I worked with a couple of old porters, Jocky Tanner and Claude Hickland. We were always grateful to pick up an extra threepence when the big trains came in. On my first day these two old porters told me where to stand on the platform when these trains arrived. They told me to cover the middle two coaches. I did this practically all week; they were getting all the tips and I was getting nothing. Suddenly the bell rang, it was the two dining cars I was patrolling and nobody got out of them.

I was working as a relief porter in the 1940s at West Pennard. It was a busy place, especially with all the cider traffic. There was an abattoir nearby run by John Bolton. On one occasion I went out with the van driver Charlie Ham and delivered some goods to him. Mr Bolton thanked us and said "I suppose you would like some meat". He asked me what I would like and I said "I don't mind, sir". He disappeared and came back with a bullock's heart all wrapped up in paper. I took this back to the station where I fastened it tightly to my bicycle and cycled all the way to Binegar where I lived. I was just going over the top of the Mendips when a police car came by and stopped. The policeman asked "what's on the back of your bike". I looked around and there was blood dripping out of the brown paper. I replied "it's a bullock's heart, officer". The policeman gave me a hard look then looked at his mate in the car and they both broke out laughing.

One day in the 1940s I was on portering duties at Midsomer Norton station. The S&D lorry came into the yard as usual and parked in the shed, the driver, who shall be nameless, gave me a wave. I had noticed a young lady sitting on the platform and thought she was waiting for a train. The lorry was now in the shed and it was my job to close the yard gates, so I picked up my handlamp and walked out and closed the gates. When I came back I looked in the shed and noticed the lorry was shaking a bit, I thought it was the driver trying to get his sheet down. I went in and lifted up the sheet and said to the driver "do you want any help" the driver replied "no, Frank, I can manage this little job on my own".

I remember when I was a guard in the 1950s I was on a train from Bournemouth to Bath. We stopped at Blandford to take water and suddenly the driver realized there was something wrong with the engine. They apparently had dropped a plug in the firebox. The best thing is to bale the fire out so not to cause further damage. The fireman was working as hard as he could to get the red hot ashes out of the firebox, he was flinging them out of the other side of the cab, not realizing that he was throwing it onto the wooden sleepers. Within a few minutes they were ablaze. Fortunately there were some permanent way men nearby who put the fire out. They had to get an assisting loco down from Templecombe, which I recall was a 4F, to haul the train into Bath.

In 1947 I remember working a train as a guard from Bath to Evercreech Junction. We had arrived at Evercreech and I was in the sidings forming up the 12.30 back to Bath. Walking up through was stationmaster Jack Pike. He was out doing a bit of rabbiting in his lunch hour and under his arm he had an air rifle. We stopped and had a chat. I happened to glance up at a tree across the field and said to Mr Pike "there's a pigeon on a branch over there". It was quite a distance away so I said "I'll give you a shilling if you can knock him down". He charged his gun, levelled up and fired, the pigeon fell to the ground, I paid up the shilling. I walked across the field and picked up this nice big plump wood pigeon; a few days later it made a nice pie which was certainly worth the shilling.

There was another stationmaster at Evercreech Junction called Bert Hobbs. One day after work Mr Hobbs came out onto the platform and said "do you fancy going down the line to get some rabbits"; he had his double-barrelled shotgun with him. About half a mile down the line I found out that he had an allotment. He did not want me there to find the rabbits, he wanted me to tidy up his allotment.

He kept me down there for about an hour and a half and finally said "no rabbits out here tonight, Frank, let's go back to the station and have a cup of tea". Mr Hobbs and myself never went rabbiting together again.

There was a driver at Bath Green Park who staff used to say that when he was driving and the moon was rising it used to affect him. I was with him on such a night in the 1950s. We had 28 coal wagons out of Bath. When we turned over the ridge at Masbury he went like a rocket. He cleared Binegar to Shepton Mallet in 14 minutes. This was too much for me, I put the handbrake hard on in the guard's van going through Evercreech New. The sparks were flying and my wheels were that hot that I could see the time on the church clock 200 yards away. When we arrived at Evercreech Junction I got out of the guard's van and walked down to him to have a few words. I said to him "is everything alright?", thinking he must have had some kind of seizure. He replied "what do you mean?" I said "I thought you were running away down the bank". He replied "don't you worry about the engine, you worry about the guard's van". We left Evercreech Junction and I put my brake hard on and left it on until we arrived at Templecombe. What a journey!

Evercreech Junction North signalbox was mysteriously burnt down on the last day of service, 5th March 1966. (*Les Willsher collection*)

A Locomotive Club of Great Britain farewell special on 5th March 1966 with two Ivatt tanks, Nos.41307 and 41269, at Evercreech Junction. (*David Walden*)

Evercreech Junction on the last weekend. Battle of Britain Pacific No.34057 *Biggin Hill* waits in the middle road, with cylinder cocks open, to assist a special train on to Bath. (*David Walden*)

BR Standard No.75007 enters Evercreech Junction. The signalbox on the right is where the well-known Les Williams worked for many years – what a character he was! (*Keith Barrett collection*)

The driver of Collett 0-6-0 No.2218 enjoys a leisurely chat with the porter at Evercreech Junction in July 1964 while a further Collett in the distance is heading southbound. Notice the chalk lettering for Acton and Ealing on the side of the van – a long way from home. (*David Walden*)

Ivatt tank No.41307 and a BR Standard No.80138 on the last Saturday before closure. The cab of 41307 is crowded with enthusiasts as it starts to move away from Evercreech Junction – note the disc with the crest of the S&DJR mounted on the bunker of the Ivatt tank. (*David Walden*)

Shunters Fred Hicks, on the left, and Philip Hatcher on duty at Evercreech Junction in the fifties in this atmospheric shot of 8F No.48471 blowing off steam. (*Keith Barrett collection*)

BR Standard No.76015 on an up train passing the goods yard entrance at Evercreech in 1966. Within a short time of this photo being taken she was condemned and scrapped at Swansea. (*Eric Rimmer*)

(*above*) Lamyatt crossing, south of Evercreech, was a Somerset Central structure. Norman and Mary Lockwood were the crossing keepers here for some time. The cottage windows are open and the washing is drying on this lovely summer day. If only these idyllic scenes were still with us today. (*David Milton*)

(*right*) The small LSWR-style wooden signalbox of Cole with its 14 levers, photographed on 21st March 1965. It was a nice spot for a signalman to spend his days operating the box and enjoying the lovely Somerset countryside. Among those who worked the box were James Gould, Sid Pitt and Norman Rallison. (*Colin Caddy*)

Cole station, looking north, in 1964. The station looks immaculate with freshly painted white lines, a credit to the staff who always took great pride in their station. (*Eric Rimmer*)

The platelaying gang at Cole in the early 1900s – hard men for a hard job. (*Keith Barrett collection*)

BR Standard No.76025 crosses the ex-GWR main line near Cole with a northbound train in July 1964. The stock is Great Western in BR maroon livery. (*David Walden*)

Roy Pitman – Passenger

Sometimes, when I am standing on Washford Station, the home of the Somerset & Dorset Railway Trust, in my uniform as stationmaster, I cast my mind back to my first and subsequent encounters with the S&D. It must have been about 1936, when I was living at South Cheriton, that I had to walk the one and a half miles, via Horsington, to Templecombe station. The purpose was to catch a train to Wincanton only three miles from home in the opposite direction, for my mother to do her shopping. There were no bus services in those days and very few people owned a car.

I well recall one particular incident with my mother, who was a good talker, and would get into conversation with anyone who happened to be in our compartment. On this occasion she didn't realize the train had stopped at Wincanton. It wasn't until I pointed out to her that the Cow & Gate factory chimney was fast disappearing behind us as the train left the station and that we shouldn't still be on it. We got off the train at the next station, Cole, and had to await a train from the other direction to eventually reach Wincanton. Little did I realise then that Cole station would become very familiar to me a few years later. From 1940 to 1945 I travelled from Templecombe to Cole every day, except for holidays, in order to attend Sexey's School at nearby Bruton.

I used to cycle from my home at South Cheriton to Templecombe, leave the bike in an outbuilding at the Royal Hotel and catch the 8.15am train. From memory it was a two-coach, non-corridor train pulled by an Armstrong or Bulldog 0-6-0 or a tank locomotive. The girls from Sunny Hill School were allocated the front coach and the boys from Sexey's the rear one.

On the return journey in the afternoon there were normally four corridor coaches, the girls being allowed to travel in the front two and the boys in the rear two. In my later years I was responsible for seeing that there was no fraternisation between the two sexes. It meant standing near the connection between the second and third coaches to stop any 'trespass' into the wrong part of the train. A certain girl from Sunny Hill had the same duties for her school – need I say that she and I became quite friendly.

Caps were a compulsory part of the school uniform and somehow they disappeared through the train windows quite regularly. I am sure the gangers on the line must have got fed up of returning them either to Cole or Templecombe for later collection. Incidentally there was a nice goldfish pond on the station at Cole where the staff used to sell the fish for the tea fund.

As a lad I didn't take a great interest in the names of the staff on the S&D but I do remember Ray Stokes as a young fireman, guard Dickie Bird and Templecombe ticket collector Cecil Gillman. If the morning train happened to have a milk tanker attached to the rear we knew that there would be a shunt at Wincanton for the Cow & Gate milk factory and that we might be late for school as a result.

Quite often homework was done on the morning train; we were far too busy with other interests to do it the previous night with the result that everyone got the same answers – as often as not incorrect.

Once in the later years of the war we had a school field trip to the peat fields on the Somerset levels and then on to Burnham-on-Sea. On the return journey, changing at Evercreech Junction and waiting for the connection to Cole, a lot of young people could be seen, capless, sitting on seats outside the Railway Hotel drinking lemonade!

In 1944 the morning train was often delayed by troop and ambulance trains following the invasion of Europe. The American soldiers were extremely generous with gifts of chocolate, gum and cigarettes. G.I.s were stationed at South Cheriton and I was able to buy packets of 20 Lucky Strike or Camel cigarettes for 4d. During the war luxuries were very scarce. Occasionally the buffet on Templecombe station would have some rather dry madeira cake which was available from Gladys for 4d per slice.

At Cole season tickets were rarely examined by the staff. Whenever they were it was inevitable that someone had forgotten theirs. I remember that the stationmaster Sidney Cox was nicknamed 'Squeaky' because he had a rather high-pitched voice and there was a signalman porter there called Fred Thick.

Going back in time our Sunday School outing was to Weymouth by train from Templecombe in pre-war days. An S&D clerk would come to the village hall and sell the rail tickets a couple of weeks in advance. The train must have been routed via Broadstone and Hamworthy, but I was too young to remember. I can remember however that it never rained, there was always bright sunshine all day and that we always took a paddle steamer trip round Portland Harbour. On the return journey in the evening we trailed paper streamers from the train windows.

Nearly all boys were trainspotters in those days and I was no exception. There was quite a variety of motive power on the S&D. Apart from the common 3F and 4F 0-6-0s, there were the 2P 4-4-0s, 7F 2-8-0s (then numbered in the 138xx series) and tank locos. There were also class 5 4-6-0s which we called Staniers not having heard the expression 'Black Five'. During the war the Southern transferred ten class S11 4-4-0s, Nos.395-404, and I believe six class T1 0-4-4Ts, Nos. 1-6, for a period to assist with a locomotive shortage.

Playing football and cricket as a lad there were often matches against Templecombe. Rivals I can recall were Brian Tanner, Cyril Read, Percy Hobbs, Reg Darke, Derek Howcutt, Gordon Hatcher, Norman Rice, Dick Rendle and Ron Hatcher. All eventually worked on the S&D. I only once travelled on the *Pines Express*. It was stopped specially at Templecombe Lower platform in order for a gang of us, including Walt Webb and Fred Brown, to go to Bath for a wartime cup tie between Bath City and Aston Villa.

My wife Mona had family connections with the S&D. Her father Bert Cluett was a lengthman and her brother Norman a fireman at Templecombe. In the same row of houses as her at Henstridge, S&D men Fred Fisher and Olaf Wiles both lived.

Roy Pitman and his wife Mona

In South Cheriton, where I spent my childhood and early youth, many of my pals joined the railway when leaving school. Some went to the Southern Railway, others to the S&D, including John Holt, Mike Fudge, Roy Nancarrow, brothers Ernie, Ken, Ray and Cliff Day, cousin Reg Day, Maurice Miles and Phil Hatcher. Older men included Jack Osborne and Fritz Lawrence. At nearby Horsington, Dick Isaacs, Stan Morey, Len Hardee, George Barrett, Jim Young, brothers Basil and Den Foot also worked on the S&D.

It is a true story that a certain fireman used to take a 12-bore shotgun on the footplate in order to take a pot at line-side rabbits to provide a dinner.

I can remember only too well the crash at Henstridge in 1944. I was told on Cole station that something had happened but no further details. Instead of cycling home from Templecombe that evening I cycled to Henstridge. It was a horrific scene and I recall one engine in a line-side field and the other a little way down the line. I still cannot understand how Peter Jackson, the porter, wasn't killed when he was toppled from the signal ladder by the train.

I was lucky to travel all over the S&D network except on the Bridgwater branch. The only time I ever went to Wells, I travelled from Templecombe with changes at Evercreech Junction and at Glastonbury, to watch Somerset play cricket.

It has been my privilege over the past decade or so to organise the now biennial re-union of ex S&D employees at Washford. As a result I have not only been able to renew many friendships but also to make many new acquaintances, far too many to name individually. Who said that "nostalgia isn't what it used to be"?

Collett 0-6-0 No. 2277 entering Cole station with a train bound for Temple-combe. Look at the bracket signal with its double finials and, of course, the platform lamps – beautiful. (*Keith Barrett collection*)

(*below*) BR Standard No.73054 running light engine near Cole in the 1960s with a full tender of coal. The fireman has taken a breather to enjoy the superb scenery on this stretch of the line. (*Eric Rimmer*)

A silent Wincanton in the sixties, looking north. This station was once a hive of activity with traffic from the Cow and Gate milk factory and the nearby Race Course. (*Keith Barrett collection*)

A group of S&D men at Wincanton in June 1950. From left to right, Eric Hamblin, Norman Rallison, Jock Bain, Win Padfield, Charlie Lethbridge, Percy Hannam, Norman Ashfield, Harry Light, Bob Rush, Arnold Linton and Norman Gould. (*Norman Rallison collection*)

Attractive Regular
EXCURSIONS

from

BATH (Green Park), RADSTOCK NORTH MIDSOMER NORTON SOUTH CHILCOMPTON, HIGHBRIDGE for BURNHAM-on-SEA, SHEPTON MALLET (Charlton Road) EVERCREECH Jct., COLE, WINCANTON and INTERMEDIATE STATIONS

10th SEPTEMBER, 1962 to 16th JUNE, 1963

(INCLUSIVE)

(OR UNTIL FURTHER NOTICE)

The Train Services in this pamphlet are subject to alteration or cancellation at short notice and do not necessarily apply at Bank or Public Holidays. Passengers should confirm beforehand the service on which they intend to travel.

BRITISH RAILWAYS

THE SOMERSET & DORSET

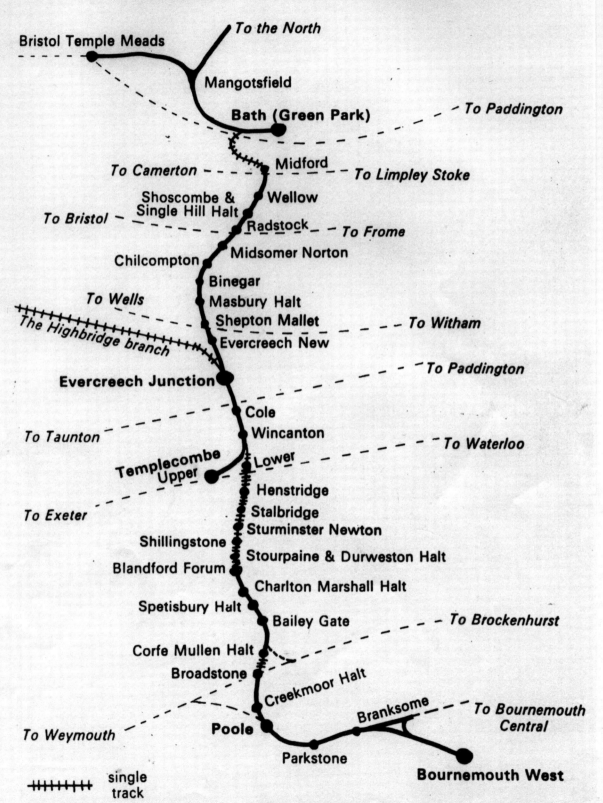

Map of the principal section of the S&D showing where other railway lines cross it. (*S&DRT collection*)

Tony Axford – Fireman

I joined the S&D in 1962 as a fireman and worked with many of the older drivers like George Welch, Den Norris, Walt Jeans, Pat Evans and Percy Hobbs. My regular mate was Les Cuss and it was with him that I once had a frightening experience. It was in 1965, our motive power was a class 2P 2-6-2 Ivatt tank engine; we were probably doing over 20mph light engine as we were approaching several sets of points. Just past No.2 box at Templecombe Les applied the full brake on our 2P and immediately realized that the steam was not going into the brake piston but it was going onto the track. The brakes had completely failed. My first instinct was to jump for it but Les shouted out to me to put the handbrake on whilst he frantically tried to put the engine into

reverse. After what seemed a lifetime I screwed the handbrake on tight, but I knew there was no way we were going to avoid a serious accident. I pleaded with Les to jump for it but he was trying for all his worth to stop the engine. In the end Les and I both had to jump for it. I was very fortunate that I had picked a relatively clear piece of ground with no tracks; as I landed I hit the ground running and just managed to stay on my feet. Looking up, to my horror I realized that our runaway engine was going to collide with another class 2P as the points were still set towards it. I noticed that its fireman David Walker was hooking up the engine for the afternoon passenger to Glastonbury. I shouted at the top of my voice to warn him and he came out

Johnson class 2P No.320 stands at Templecombe in S&D platform No.3 in 1931 beside the original LSWR signalbox. Harry Steele worked this box in the 1930s. In 1938 the entire station, including this box, was re-modelled in Southern style (see the photograph on the next page). (*Andrew Fisher collection*)

just as though he was diving into a swimming pool. I don't blame him as I estimated that he had about three seconds before he would have been seriously injured. Immediately after our engine hit his, I remember a massive amount of steam, water and dust flying everywhere. The thing that most stuck in my mind was that some lumps of coal flew out of the top of the bunker. This was amazing as it was virtually empty at the time and emphasized the force of the impact. Unfortunately when Les jumped he landed badly and was off work for some time. He had stayed on the engine right till the end which was quite a brave act. I seem to remember that both engines were unrepairable.

One rather bizarre thing happened one day when we were climbing out of Bath towards Devonshire Tunnel. We were on a passenger train but going quite slowly as was normal on this climb when I spotted two dogs playing in the middle of our single track. As we approached them they didn't seem at all worried at first but as we got closer they started to trot on in front giving an occasional glance back. This went on for a while and as we gradually got closer they became a bit more concerned and speeded up. By this time we were getting into a deeper and deeper cutting. Now they were beginning to get really worried and tired; one made a bolt for it and scrambled up the steep embankment, the other one carried on until it was past the point of no return and to our amazement ran into the dark tunnel. To this day I would like to think that it cowered down inside the tunnel as we passed by and trotted back out safe and sound when we had gone, but I guess I will never know.

4F No.44523 awaits departure from S&D No.3 platform at Templecombe with a northbound train in the early 1960s. In the foreground is the bridge over the main road, over which the platform has been extended. Behind the photographer the track runs down to the Lower Yard. (*Andrew Fisher collection*)

(*left*) Templecombe fireman Gerald Trowbridge in his well-kept garden in the 1950s, ready to go to work. His father, Frank, was a porter at Sturminster Newton and features in the photo on page 95. (*Gerald Trowbridge collection*)

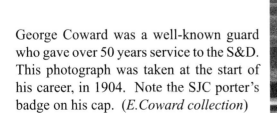

George Coward was a well-known guard who gave over 50 years service to the S&D. This photograph was taken at the start of his career, in 1904. Note the SJC porter's badge on his cap. (*E.Coward collection*)

The permanent way gang at Templecombe near No.2 Junction in the early 1900s. From left to right, Harold Coffin, Bob Elkins, Walt Rolls, Charlie Cook, Bill Candy, Ted Bennett and Fred Foot. (*Keith Barrett collection*)

S&D railwaymen at Templecombe in the fifties – from left to right, Henry Webber, Walt Webb, Bert Rolls, Ken Arnott and Ern Cawley. (*Keith Barrett collection*)

Templecombe permanent way gang in the fifties – from left to right, Fred Thorne, Archie Sutton, Fred Brown (goods checker), Jess Hiscock, Pete Moreton and Charlie Coffin. (*Gordon Hatcher collection*)

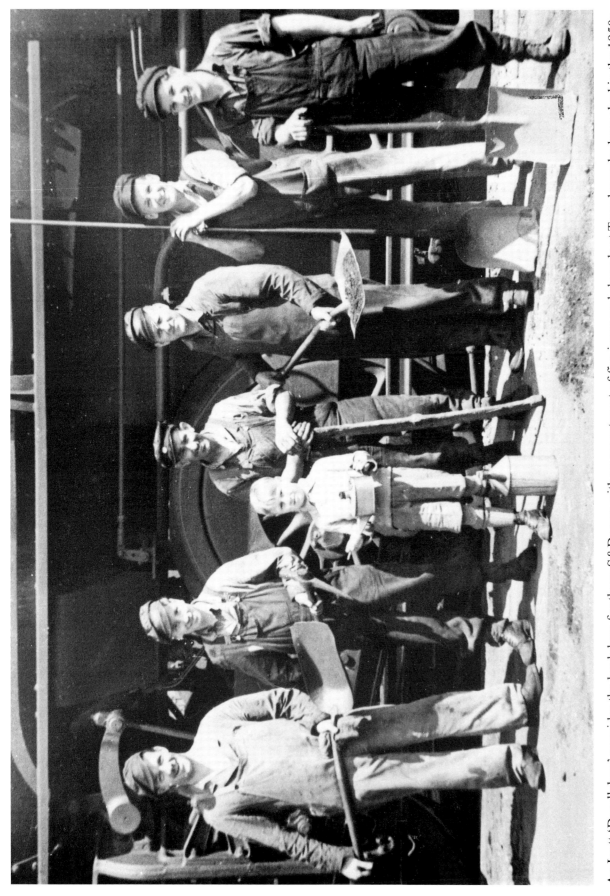

An Ivatt 'Doodlebug' provides the backdrop for these S&D men with an assortment of fire irons and shovels at Templecombe loco shed in the 1950s. From left to right, Ray Stokes, Cliff Day, Ern Cawley, Jack Hix, Gordon Hatcher and Bob Fisher – the young lad is George Cawley. (*Gordon Hatcher collection*)

Templecombe fitters. from left to right, Bert Hughes, Frank Iley and Arthur Elliott, with a rather dirty 7F No.53808 (now preserved by the S&D Trust at Washford). (*Peter Pike collection*)

(*above*) Fitter Norman Penaligon resting against BR Standard No.76063 at Templecombe in March 1963. (*Peter Pike collection*)

(*left*) Fireman Fred Fisher, left, and driver Dick Rendle look happy on the footplate of Collett 0-6-0 No.2223 at Templecombe in the 1960s. (*Fred Fisher collection*)

A Home Counties Railway Society special at No.2 box at Templecombe on 7th June 1964. The driver on 7F No.53807 was Alwyn Hannam with fireman Don Garrett, and on the 4F, No.44558, was Fred Fisher with fireman Bruce Briant. (*Percy Hobbs collection*)

An engine spotter's special from Bournemouth to Salisbury via Templecombe in 1965 – Fowler 7F No.53804 has driver Bert Jones and fireman Derek Howcutt on the footplate of this South Western Limited train. (*Derek Howcutt collection*)

7F No.53804 at Templecombe No.2 with a down special for the Stephenson Locomotive Society on 11th September 1960. Driver Len West is looking out of his cab. (*Keith Barrett collection*)

1P No.58086, with a Highbridge to Templecombe train, nearing its destination on 14th September 1957. (*R.E.Toop*)

4F No.44560 bustles away from Templecombe with a Bath-bound train on 23rd August 1952. (*R.E.Toop*)

2P No.40601 departing Templecombe with a midday train for Bath in the early 1950s. (*R.E.Toop*)

(*above*) 4F No.44422 (now preserved) has just arrived at Templecombe No.3 platform with a southbound train in July 1964. (*Andrew Fisher collection*)

(*below left*) 2P No.524 light engine in front of a fine array of signals at Templecombe Junction on 6th July 1938. Note No.2 signalbox behind the tender. (*H.C.Casserley*)

(*below right*) BR Standard No.80138 somewhat optimistically carries a Waterloo destination board as it stands in Templecombe No.3 platform. It headed the last S&D train to Bournemouth Central on 5th March 1966. (*David Walden*)

An inviting welcome into Henstridge station on a sunny day in the 1960s. For such a small station it boasted a ladies and gents waiting room and a booking office. (*Eric Rimmer*)

Henstridge station in the 1930s. From left to right, Peter Jackson, Joe Coward and stationmaster Alan Whitehead are manoeuvring castings with the station crane. (*E.Coward collection*)

The driver of 2P No.40569 is eager to move off as parcels are being loaded by the porters at Stalbridge in the 1950s. (*Mike Baker collection*)

The end is near – some sleepers have already lost their rails as Merchant Navy class No.35011 *General Steam Navigation* pulls into Stalbridge on 1st January 1966 with an LCGB Mendip Merchantman Rail Tour. (*Colin Caddy*)

Driver Trevor Netley, left, and fireman Mike Baker at Stalbridge ready to depart with BR Standard No.76026 on 5th March 1966. (*Mike Baker collection*)

South Western & Midland Railway Companies' SOMERSET & DORSET JOINT LINE.

[182.]
N 7; 10,000.

NEWSPAPER PARCELS WAY BILL.
(TO BE USED ONLY FOR TRAFFIC AT THE NEWSPAPER SCALE.)

Guards' Signatures.

From _Shillingstone_ to _Stalbridge_

via

Departure _1/3_ o'clock Train _10_ day of _9_ 190 _3_

Nos. must not be abstracted.	NAME.	DESTINATION.	Weight. lbs.	Value of Labels.		TRAFFIC NOT LABELLED.						
						PAID ON.		To Pay.			PAID.	
				s.	d.	s.	d.	£	s.	d.	£	s.	d.
	Bordeaux			1								
	_13_											
	_2166_											

N.B.—The Guard of the Train must see that the entries on this Bill correspond with the Parcels delivered to and given up by him.

Sturminster Newton station in 1952. The dip in the platform was for passengers to cross the line as there was no footbridge. The weekly markets gave much needed revenue to the station. (*Eric Rimmer*)

From left to right, Don Page, Jack Bell, Maurice Stacey, Ted Drew, stationmaster Sidney Cox and Frank Trowbridge pose for a team photo at Sturminster Newton in the 1960s. (*Gerald Trowbridge collection*)

(*left*) Another LSWR-style wooden signalbox at Sturminster Newton in 1966 – the fire buckets have gone and the tablet catcher stands idle. Signalmen Ivor Hardwich and Peter Stephens worked this box in the good times. (*Colin Caddy*)

(*below*) Driver Walt Jeans and fireman Ernie Hunt on a rather smoky BR Standard No.82039 with the up 'milky' from Bailey Gate at Hammoon Overbridge (bridge No.176) between Sturminster Newton and Shillingstone. Hopefully no ladies had hung their washing out nearby. (*Keith Barrett collection*)

(*right*) Shillingstone station on a beautiful sunny day. It looks immaculate, with flat bottom rails laid on up and down roads. I hope the photographer remembered to pick up his spare camera. (*Eric Rimmer*)

(*below*) Shillingstone's wooden 16-lever signal-box was situated on the up platform by the goods yard. George Ainsworth was the 'bobby' here for many years. This 1960s shot shows the motorized engineer's trolley shelter on the left. The goods dock with the discarded oil drums is on the right. (*Eric Rimmer*)

Shillingstone staff, who between them gave over 150 years service to the S&D, photographed at Christmas 1965; from left to right, stationmaster Ken Davey, porters Wilf Savory and Reg Eaton, lorry driver Bert Sherlock, ganger Albert Snook, booking clerk Don Ridout, signalmen Harold Hooper, Bert Scammell and Alan Cox. (*Colin Caddy collection*)

Signalman George Ainsworth and his wife Cicely receiving gifts from his workmates to reward 50 years loyal service on the S&D. They include Len Farley, Bob Downes, Ivor Ridout, Roy Yates, Ron Jackson, Don Ridout, Wilf Savory, Alan Cox, stationmaster Ken Forester, Don May, Jack Bell, Bert Scammell, Reg Eaton, Bill Dyer and Jim Maidment. They were photographed on 18th December 1965 at Shillingstone box. (*Bob Downes collection*)

(*above left*) Signalman George Ainsworth stands proudly on the veranda of Shillingstone box where he worked for many years. (*Bob Downes collection*)

(*above right*) Porter Bob Downes on the up platform at Shillingstone in 1963. He later became a signalman at Corfe Mullen. (*Bob Downes collection*)

(*left*) The firemen are getting younger and younger – John Sawyer with driver Ben Ford, left, at Shillingstone on a holiday special with BR Standard No.73001 from Bath to Bournemouth on 30th August 1965. (*Richard Clayton*)

2P No.40537 with BR Standard No.73050 (now preserved) waits in the down loop at Shillingstone as another BR Standard, No.73019, arrives with an up train in the 1950s. (*Keith Barrett collection*)

A stopping train to Templecombe, hauled by 2P 40696 with a Southern 3-coach set and 'guv' at the rear, prepares to stop at Shillingstone. (*Keith Barrett collection*)

BR Standard No.76011 dashes through the Dorset countryside between Stourpaine and Shillingstone with a northbound train in the mid-sixties. (*David Walden*)

4-4-0 No.14 hauling a train of five vehicles near Blandford, c.1898. This locomotive had been built at Derby in 1897 so was comparatively new – what a splendid sight it must have been in S&D blue. (*Keith Barrettt collection*)

The British Young Travellers' Society ran a Hampshire Explorer special in 1967, seen here standing at Blandford Forum with BR Standard No.77014, the only such loco on the Southern, gently blowing off steam. (*David Walden*)

A derailment of a coal train at Blandford St Mary Bridge, just south of Blandford Forum station, on 6th March 1929 – quite a spectacle for the watching crowd on top of the bridge. (*Harold Whiting collection*)

A spring day at Blandford Forum with everything looking neat and tidy. A GWR Pannier tank engine is in the sidings with some goods wagons. It is hard to imagine as you look at this 1960s photograph that this station is now covered by a housing estate. (*Eric Rimmer*)

Porter Fred Dominey stands in the Blandford station yard with one of the shunting horses in 1920. Fred spent 45 years on the S&D. (*Bob Downes collection*)

S&D road wagons, loaded with food containers made by W.Pond & Son of Blandford for the forces in the 1914-18 war, are paraded with staff outside Blandford Parish Church. (*Bob Downes collection*)

The legendary driver Donald Beale, left, with his fireman Peter Smith aboard BR Standard No.73051 on the up *Pines* at Blandford Forum. (*Donald Beale collection*)

Blandford Forum signalbox, once struck by lightning and destroyed by fire, was rebuilt and survived to the end. It is seen here in 1962. Arthur Bowen was its resident signalman – how many times did he climb those stairs? (*Eric Rimmer*)

BLANDFORD SIGNAL BOX. STRUCK BY LIGHTNING

(*above*) Blandford Forum signalbox after it was struck and set alight by lightning at 10.45pm on 23rd June 1906.
(*below left*) The inside of the signalbox showing the charred remains. Fortunately the signalman, Charles Whiting, escaped and nobody was hurt in this incident.
(*below right*) The signalbox on fire, seen from a nearby roof. (*all photos L.Stickley*)

BLANDFORD SIGNAL BOX. STRUCK BY LIGHTNING   JUNE 23 1906

Harold 'Nobby' Whiting was an S&D man all his life which started in 1927. He ended his career at Blandford as a porter and was the last railwayman to close the gates there on 6th January 1969. (*Maud Whiting collection*)

(*below*) BR Standard No.82039 seen near Spetisbury with the 4.45pm Bailey Gate-Templecombe train on 10th July 1959. The track looks immaculate – well done to the permanent way gang. (*R.C.Riley*)

Reg Darke – Driver

I have driven many different locomotives on the S&D since I started at Templecombe in 1940. The 7Fs and LMS 3Fs were the best workhorses for the S&D system although the 4Fs carried most of the heavier passenger work before the arrival of the Black Fives and then the Southern & GWR locos. The 4Fs were not very popular with the crews because they were not good steamers, they would not coast freely down inclines. They coasted with a monotonous clacking noise from the snifting valve that opened to prevent pressure in the cylinder and cause damage. To open this valve the driver, when coasting, wound the reversing lever below the D position marked on the guide. I recall an occasion when a driver failed to do so and bent the side rod. I think it was No.44559.

Our 4F at Templecombe was 4417, later having another 4 added. She covered all special excursion trains locally. This engine spent all her life at Templecombe and never left except for overhauls to Derby. If I had been asked to save one 4F from the scrapyard she would have been my first choice. Sadly she was scrapped at Derby in May 1963.

Probably the one engine that is spoken about the most is the 2-8-0 7F series and I have had the privilege of driving all eleven 7Fs. This is my short summing up of them.

53800/1 ... Both these engines were good to work with, the only problem was that the piston glands would very often blow, causing you to lose power and of course the engine would not pull properly.

53802 ... A good one for steam but when it came back after being overhauled at Derby works she was only back in service for a few weeks when the driving gear would revolve with excessive clanking noises. I felt sorry for the residents of the nearby houses along the line, especially on the night Poole goods when going light engine to Branksome Triangle for turning at 1.00am in the early morning.

53803 ... An excessive water user; the reason for this was that the blowdown valve was wasting vital water from the boiler. This valve worked when the regulator was opened to remove impurities from the boiler water surface to escape at the rear of the tender which was supposedly to allow the boiler to go longer between washouts.

53804 ... I never had any problems, she must have liked my handling. Some of my workmates complained of her not steaming well.

53805 ... I would say the best of the right-handed earlier models, a good workhorse.

53806 ... The first of the later left-hand drive models with a large boiler, we always had a good trip with this one.

53807/8 ... The two best 7Fs in my opinion just like twins.

53809 ... comparable to 53804; must have had her off days for steaming problems, but never gave me any troubles.

53810 ... Without a doubt this was the poorest of these great engines. For some unknown reason there was nobody who could set the valves properly on this one to last very long. The result was irregular exhaust beats and a sideways rocking movement, much worse when working tender first of which we did quite a lot. This meant you could not obtain an early point of cut off which means, in effect, the same as driving a motorcar in low gear when requiring higher speeds.

One driving memory I can recall was on 17th September 1956. We were working the 4.10pm from Evercreech to Bournemouth on 2P No.40696, and my fireman was Basil Foot. This train was the connection for passengers off the *Pines Express* for stations to Shillingstone. On this particular evening we stopped at Charlton Marshall Halt and picked up a family of four who alighted at Spetisbury Halt, the next stop along. They then wanted to go over the other side of the platform. The guard had to conduct them across the track. I asked the guard later what they were playing at; he replied that they wanted to take their two young children on the last train. We were the last down train and the 5.18pm was the last up train to stop at the halts. The facts had not sunk in that it was the last official stop at these halts; they were closed that day.

I worked with and met many of the old-time drivers at Templecombe in my 26 years on the S&D. Drivers like Charlie Stokes, Len Counsell, Len Dutton, of course my father Bill Darke, Arthur Hatcher, Fred Marshall and many more.

(*left*) Edward Ham, stationmaster at Shapwick and later at Bailey Gate, photographed in the early 1900s. He was an S&D railwayman for 46 years. (*John Badman collection*)

(*below*) 4F No.44557 steams north past the small wooden signalbox of Bailey Gate on 4th July 1961. This box was kept very busy with milk traffic from United Dairies which had its own siding. In 1881 the first full-time signalman was Charles Summers and when the box closed it was Fred Willis. (*R.C.Riley*)

(*above*) Bath Green Park guard Bert Veasey waves the green flag at Bailey Gate in November 1963. This was a very busy station, not only with the milk traffic but also with watercress – many a footplate crew has eaten his cheese sandwiches with a wadding of Bailey Gate watercress. (*Martin Veasey collection*)

(*right*) BR Standard No.76026 passing Corfe Mullen on 16th October 1966 with a Locomotive Club of Great Britain special. The railway cottage on the left used to be occupied by George Ridout and his wife – he was a ganger on the S&D in the 1920s. (*Bob Downes collection*)

Broadstone on 22nd September 1963, where S&D lines ended – the run into Bournemouth was then on LSWR metals. The footbridge rather dominates the station. Note Broadstone Hotel on the right. (*Colin Caddy*)

7F No.53807 heading for Bournemouth with an Ian Allan Severn Wessex Express special at Broadstone on 14th May 1960. (*Colin Caddy*)

The station looks forlorn as driver Pat Evans chats with fireman Dave Walters at Broadstone. BR Standard No.73052 was withdrawn in 1964. (*Keith Barrett collection*)

BR Standard No.76028 passes Broadstone signalbox in 1958. The LSWR brick box had 32 levers and controlled the junction and sidings. Brian Baggs was the last signalman on duty when it closed. (*Colin Caddy*)

BR Standard No.73051 passing Broadstone distant signal with the 1.10pm Bournemouth to Bristol train. (*Keith Barrett collection*)

Bournemouth West with its six platforms, seen on 3rd July 1961. It was the terminus for the S&D. Reg Darke was the last S&D driver to take a train out of this station when it closed for S&D traffic in 1965. (*Colin Caddy*)

The last *Pines Express* to leave Bournemouth West on 8th September 1962 with 9F No.92220 *Evening Star*. *(David Walden collection)*

Driver George Morley, left, and fireman Bruce Briant gaze happily from the cab at Bournemouth West while waiting to take the 5.30pm to Templecombe with Ivatt tank No.41243. *(Bruce Briant collection)*

THE
RAILWAY CORRESPONDENCE AND TRAVEL SOCIETY

ITINERARY

OF THE

SOMERSET AND DORSET FAREWELL RAIL TOUR

WATERLOO · SOUTHAMPTON · BOURNEMOUTH · EVERCREECH

HIGHBRIDGE · BRISTOL (TEMPLE MEADS) · BATH (GREEN PARK)

EVERCREECH · TEMPLECOMBE · SALISBURY · WATERLOO

SUNDAY, 6th MARCH, 1966

It is the end of the line for Pylle station, the first on the branch. The last train has passed, the platform is full of weeds and the passing loop has been removed. But although the A37 road bridge has now vanished, the memory still lives on, as does the goods shed which is now converted into a family home. (*Eric Rimmer*)

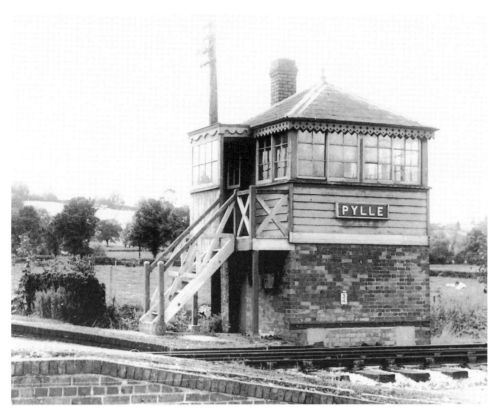

(*left*) Pylle signalbox still had its fire buckets in 1956 as this photograph shows. Unfortunately this grand structure was only used after 1929 as a ground frame for the single siding to the goods shed. Ern Skuse was one of the last porter/signalmen here – many a tomato plant grew in the signalbox thanks to Ern. (*R.M.Casserley*)

(*below*) Fireman Dick Isaacs exchanges tablets with the signalman at West Pennard on Collett 0-6-0 No.2277 hauling the Highbridge 'market'. (*Keith Barrett collection*)

(*right*) The neat station of West Pennard looking east towards Evercreech. The mainstay of the station was the cider traffic from local producers. Most of the buildings are still intact with the booking office and waiting room lived in by a lovely couple – looking at this 1950 photo you wish the S&D was alive and well. (*Lens of Sutton*)

(*below*) Wells Priory Road station once boasted an overall roof but this was removed after the S&D closed. The line to Glastonbury forked to the left in the middle distance. The line through the station was the GWR's Wells branch from Yatton to Witham Friary, its station at Wells being Tucker Street. (*Author's collection*)

EACH WEEKDAY
To Glastonbury and Highbridge for Burnham-on-Sea

FROM	DEPART		RETURN FARE, SECOND CLASS	
			Glastonbury	Highbridge for Burnham-on-Sea
	a.m.	p.m.	s. d.	s. d.
BATH (Green Park)	8a 15	—	9/0	12/0
MIDFORD	8a 26	—	8/0	11/0
WELLOW	8a 33	—	7/3	10/3
SHOSCOMBE & SINGLE HILL HT.	8a 37	—	6/9	9/9
RADSTOCK NORTH	8a 43	—	6/3	9/3
MIDSOMER NORTON SOUTH ...	8a 50	—	5/9	8/9
CHILCOMPTON	8a 58	—	5/3	8/3
BINEGAR	9a 6	—	4/6	7/6
SHEPTON MALLET (Charlton Rd.)	9a 18	—	3/3	6/3
EVERCREECH NEW	9a 24	—	3/0	5/6
WINCANTON	9a 14	—	4/6	7/0
COLE	9a 22		3/9	6/0
EVERCREECH JUNCTION ...	9 55	1 15	2/9	5/3
PYLLE HALT	10 0	1 20	2/6	5/0
WEST PENNARD	10 8	1 28	2/0	4/3
GLASTONBURY & STREET arr.	10 20	1 40		
HIGHBRIDGE for BURNHAM-ON-SEA ... arr.	10 51	2 12		

Return by any train the same day affording a service through to destination.
The Bristol Omnibus Company operate buses from Highbridge for Burnham-on-Sea to Burnham-on-Sea.

a—Change at Evercreech Jct.   SX—Saturdays excepted.   SO—Saturdays only.

EACH WEEKDAY
To WESTON-S-MARE

FROM	DEPART	RETURN FARE SECOND CLASS	ARRIVAL ON RETURN
	a.m.	s. d.	p.m.
EVERCREECH JUNCTION ...	8 15	7/6	8 9
WEST PENNARD	8 25	6/6	7 53
GLASTONBURY and STREET ...	8 36	5/6	7 42
ASHCOTT	8 42	5/0	7 32
SHAPWICK	8 47	4/6	7 27
EDINGTON BURTLE	8 52	4/0	7 22
BASON BRIDGE	8 58	3/6	7 14
WESTON-S-MARE ... arr.	9 33		

Return from Weston-super-Mare at 6-28 p.m. the same day.
Change at Highbridge for Burnham-on-Sea in both directions.

Glastonbury station looking towards West Pennard with its island platform canopy. This survived and now covers the town's open-air market. The main traffic here was from C & J Clark, shoe manufacturers of Street. (*Lens of Sutton*)

Ivatt tank No.41291 stands under the footbridge at Glastonbury while station staff load mail bags onto the train. (*Stan Blacker collection*)

A wet Glastonbury station in the 1950s, but the staff look happy: (back row, from left to right) Charlie Bradley, unknown, Percy Bishop, Ern Napper, Arthur Blackborough, Ted Billet; (middle row) Leslie Humphries, Fred Lester, Sam Bailey, Ron Jones, Bill Milton, Ted Cook, Fred Nicholls, Ern Pike; (front row) William Crowther, Bert Rodd, Charlie Jones, Harry Preator. (*Fred Lester collection*)

Driver Harry Pearce standing next to a 3F at Glastonbury before taking a passenger train to Highbridge in the 1950s. Harry joined in 1913 as a call boy and gave 50 years service to the S&D. (*Joyce Bell collection*)

Joyce Miles sitting on Cemetary Lane gates, on the north-east side of Glastonbury, in the 1950s where she was the crossing keeper – what a wonderful job she did. Her husband Eric was a signalman at Wells Priory Road and Glastonbury, having started at Blandford Forum. (*Eric Miles*)

Bath Green Park shedmaster, Harold Morris, right, with driver Bill May and young fireman John Baker on a cold and frosty day in December 1965 at Glastonbury station. Ivatt tank No.41223 stands in the platform. (*Bill May collection*)

S&D railwaymen pose with the last train from Glastonbury to Wells on 29th October 1951. The loco is Johnson 0-4-4T No.58086 with Midland push-pull coach M24465. On the engine, from left to right, are foreman Hugh Durston, fireman Clarence Rawles and driver Frank Banwell. In the front row are porter Harry Curtis, foreman Bill Milton, unknown, relief porter Alfred Lilley, guard Bob Fry and his son Paul Fry, the booking clerk. (*Paul Fry collection*)

(*above*) Fred Parsons stands with a shunting pole at Glastonbury yard – 3F No.43216 has a full tender of coal for the journey back down the branch. (*Fred Parsons collection*)

CENTENARY

1854 - 19

(*left*) Driver Bill Peck, left, and fireman Maurice Cook don beards to greet local dignitaries before taking out the Somerset Central Railway Centenary special on 28th August 1954. (*Maurice Cook collection*)

The 5th March 1966 Locomotive Club of Great Britain special leaving Glastonbury – the drivers of the two Ivatt tanks were Bill May on No.41307 and George Wheadon on No.41269 (*Bill May collection*)

Two Ivatt tanks again, bringing LCGB Mendip Merchantman Rail Tour into Glastonbury in January 1966. The pilot is No.41307 and the train engine No.41283 with driver Les Cuss and fireman Bruce Briant. (*Keith Barrett collection*)

(*above*) On a lovely summer's day, 6th July 1959, the 2.20pm ex Highbridge, with Ivatt tank No.41296 and four coaches, makes her way across the Somerset levels near Glastonbury. (*R.C.Riley*)

(*left*) From left to right, Maurice Mogg (Tom's son), an inspector at Crewe, with porter Hubert Rice and the famous signalman Tom Mogg (after whom the local inn is named). They were great friends and work-mates at Edington. This photo was taken in 1946 outside Chilton Drove Crossing where Hubert lived with his wife Agnes, the crossing keeper. (*John Rice collection*)

On 19th August 1949, in foggy conditions, 3F No.3260, with a freight train, collided with a small engine carrying peat from Eclipse Peat Company which was crossing the line between Shapwick and Ashcott. Driver Ray Stokes and fireman Sid Boussey leapt from the 3F as it plunged into the rhine; the guard was George Coward. The engine could not be extricated and was cut up on site. The young lad on the right-hand side of the tender is junior porter John Rice. (*Douglas Allen collection*)

John Rice – Porter

I was born in the crossing house at Stone End which is at the bottom of Cossington Bank on the Bridgwater line. I was only a few months old when the family moved to Chilton Drove Crossing where Agnes, my mother, was the crossing keeper. The cottage is still there today. It was very small with no facilities. My mother got four hours off a week and a free pass to go onto the train to Bridgwater to do her weekly shopping. The crossing was near Edington where my father Hubert worked as a porter.

My first memory of the branch was seeing the night freight arriving from Bridgwater; it was always fully loaded and brought the day's goods into Edington. Some of the drivers who carried out this turn were Charlie King, Lou Moxey, Bert Hansford and Frank Braund. On one occasion this train hit a herd of cows at Cossington and killed several of them. They were owned by farmer Mr. Coombes. One of the cows landed in the middle of the track further up the line. Patrolman Walt Clark cut out the cow's heart, put it in his bag and took it home and cooked it. Walt used to patrol the track from Bridgwater to Edington. On the way to Edington he would lay some snares to catch rabbits and then pick up what he had trapped on the way back.

Following in my parents' footsteps I left Burtle School at 14 and joined the S&D on Christmas Eve 1946, first as a junior porter at Edington Burtle for a month. Arthur Beakes was the stationmaster and he was a gentleman. I earned £1.13.4 (£1.66) per week. There were three porters, two signalmen and a clerk working there. Unfortunately my father passed away soon after I started work.

I then moved to Bason Bridge for three years where the stationmaster was Albert Coombes and the clerk Charlie Jones. When Mr Coombes moved on, the next stationmaster had another little job on the side running an ice cream cart. Most of my duties were involved with the milk factory next to the station.

I next returned to Edington where my duties consisted of operating a set of gates at the bottom of the station, keeping the platform and station buildings nice and clean and, of course, helping the passengers. I recall one day that the innkeeper of the *Burtle Inn* came back from Bridgwater with a box of chicks under one arm and a carpet under the other. He opened the carriage door, the carpet got caught in it and he fell out with all the chicks escaping from their box. We chased them everywhere and eventually got them all back safe and sound.

My days as a porter at Edington were idyllic, a country station, views over the moors and on a clear day you could see Glastonbury Tor in the distance. Mother used to walk down the track and bring me my sandwiches for dinner (there were no trains between 11.30am and 2.00pm). She wasn't supposed to leave the gates but the stationmaster used to turn a blind eye to this. Munching my sandwiches, drinking my tea and watching all the birds flying onto the nearby rhine was great for a young country lad.

One memory that stayed in my mind was when a 3F No.3260 with Ray Stokes and Sid Boussey on the footplate collided with a peat train near Ashcott, derailing the 3F which was cut up on site. I was carrying out my duties at the time when the call came through. Mr Beakes immediately went to the scene with other railway staff. I got a call sometime later from Mr Beakes, he was hungry and wanted his sandwiches. I hopped onto the breakdown train and headed towards the crash; it was a hive of activity. Some of us had our photo taken behind the stricken engine, what excitement for a junior porter!

After a period of time I decided I wanted to get on to the footplate. I had my wish and started as a cleaner at Highbridge which I really enjoyed. I had a railway bike and part of the job was knocking up footplate crews for the early morning shift. The area I covered around Highbridge was Newtown, Poplar Estate and Burnham Road.

I moved on to be a passed cleaner and finally a fireman. My driver was one of the best known men on the branch, Ronald (Chummy) Andrews. I was his mate for seven years and we never had a cross word in all that time. One of his hobbies was beekeeping and I often had a free jar of honey.

One day, I remember, we were on a class 4 excursion train from Highbridge to Bournemouth. Going up the bank at Pylle the blast pipe in the smokebox blew out. We just managed to get to Evercreech Junction and changed over to a class 7F. Pylle Bank was a beautiful sight in the summer and if you went slow enough you could pick the filbert nuts from the hanging trees. Along the bank as far as the eyes could see was a haven of flowers and wildlife. Unfortunately one day we caught a cornfield alight charging up the bank on a class 3. Fortunately it was put out pretty quickly by the local fire brigade. We always tried to be careful but this happened sometimes.

On one occasion I was firing to Bert (Sergeant) Hansford on a goods train from Highbridge to Glastonbury. Near West Pennard, Sergeant said "in a second I shall slow her down, you get down on the step where a farmer is going to give you a big bag of plums". I made a grab for the bag which I caught, then disaster, I dropped the bag and the plums went all over the ballast. The Sarg was not very happy – no plum pie for him.

The old carriage and wagon works at Highbridge was turned into a piggery after it closed. Sometime later it was used for repairing box wagons. It had four roads going into the building. One night it caught alight; there were 60 wagons in there and after the fire was put out all you had left was their skeletons of iron frames and axles.

Looking back at my life, my days on the S&D were the best by far. In fact the S&D brought me up; it was my life. I used to live to go to work, coal dust, oil it didn't bother me. Working on the branch with my mates was all I wanted, great mates like Percy and Fred Parsons, Ken Burrows, Eric Powell, Bill Pike and Will Locke.

In 1966 my love affair with the S&D was coming to an end. My mother's job at the crossing was made redundant; there was no pension or support and she had to pay rent on the cottage and with no job she was devastated.

I went to work at Bason Bridge Milk Factory, but it wasn't the same. The S&D was in my blood but I still have my memories of working across the Somerset levels on the good old S&D.

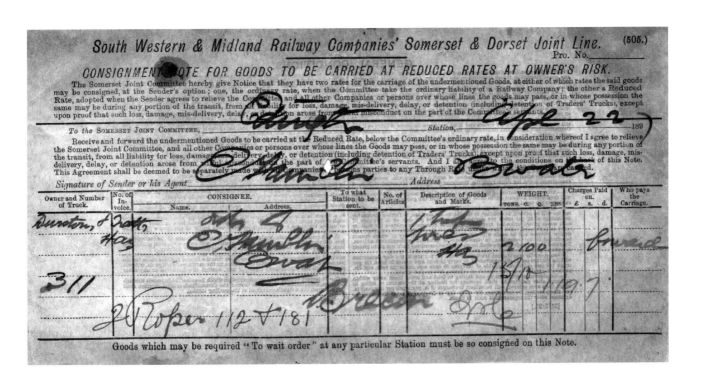

1P No.58086 drifts into Edington Junction from Highbridge on its way to Evercreech in the 1950s. (*Will Locke collection*)

(*above left*) Signalman Harry Sweetland, left, and porter Percy Parsons at Edington in 1941. (*Percy Parsons collection*)

(*above right*) Brian Wilton, the youngest railwayman on the line, dressed as an SJC guard to celebrate VE Day 1945 at Burtle village hall, Edington. (*Fred Parsons collection*)

(*left*) Bridgwater railwayman Will Locke at Cossington station – he gave many years of loyal service to the S&D. (*Will Locke collection*)

(*right*) Flooding on the Somerset levels as a class 1 passenger tank engine nears Edington Junction up home signal in the 1920s. (*Author's collection*)

(*below*) Ivatt tank No.41249 crosses Cripps Bridge between Bason Bridge and Edington with a single coach and luggage van. (*Maurice Cook collection*)

The Bridgwater Allotments Association excursion train on its return to Bridgwater from Blackpool in the early 1900s with Fowler 0-6-0 No.22 and Midland coaching stock. Signalman Reg Seviour was one of the organisers of the Allotments Association specials over the years. (*Author's collection*)

A desolate winter picture of Bridgwater station yard taken in December 1953, with the church just showing through in the middle of the photograph. Nothing moves and the station is silent. (*Dennis Ashill collection*)

(*above*) Collett 0-6-0 No.3210 leaving Bason Bridge by the side of the River Brue with a Highbridge to Templecombe stopping train. (*R.E.Toop*)

(*right*) Driver Maurice Cook, right, and fireman Keith Conibeer lean out of the cab of 3F No.43194 at Bason Bridge in 1950, with a train bound for Highbridge. (*Maurice Cook collection*)

On a sunny day in the 1950s a railwayman walks over the line at Highbridge Crossing West box which controlled S&D traffic across the main GWR line. Further along on the left is Highbridge East B box. Signalmen who controlled the West box at its zenith were Frank Jones and Aubrey Lee while the B box was looked after by Bill Allingham and Ray Parsons. (*Author's collection*)

Highbridge S&D station in the Edwardian era. The young ladies and their chaperons seem to be changing trains, possibly on to the GWR station. The lady in the foreground is fortunate to have a porter carry her case. (*Lens of Sutton*)

Highbridge works foremen's annual outing to the coast in a charabanc, c.1920 – why not by train? (*Bill May collection*)

A day out for a group of Highbridge men from the works, photographed at Highbridge station in 1926 – how smart they look. From left to right, W.Styles, C.Washer, J.Bailey, H.Luke, T.Fletcher, F.Miller, W.Brewer, J.Lewis, Sam Lane, R.Harvey, S. Washer, J.Fouracre, W.Dyer. *(Sam Lane collection)*

Staff at Highbridge, c.1900. Is the gentleman in the flat cap really a railwayman? Note the South East and Chatham board showing holiday spots on the Kent coast. (*Fred Parsons collection*)

The retirement of Alfred Whitaker, S&D locomotive superintendent from 1889 to 1911. This photo was taken in one of the shops at Highbridge works on 24th July 1911. (*Bill May collection*)

Signalman George Dewfall on the steps of Highbridge B box in 1948 – George started on the S&D in 1894 as a porter at Sturminster Newton and was one of the longest serving employees of the company, retiring from full-time work in 1946. (*Roy Cox collection*)

The S&D Railway Home Guard stand proudly in their uniforms at Highbridge in 1943. Back row, from left to right, Frank Jones, Ern Cook, Harry Miller; front row, Maurice Cook, Tom Day and Wilf Rowden. (*Maurice Cook collection*)

From left to right, fireman Fred Meaker, lady porter Kit Wheadon and driver George Brooks enjoy having their photo taken on a sunny day in 1944 at Highbridge station. (*Joyce Bell collection*)

S&D ladies Phyllis Baker, left, and Kit Wheadon, right, in their uniforms. The lady in the middle is Norah Lush. Phyllis and Kit were lady porters in the war years and Norah a clerk. This photo was taken in 1945 at Highbridge station. (*Joyce Bell collection*)

The very last passenger train in the timetable to leave Highbridge on 5th March 1966 was driven by Clarence Rawles with Tony Rossiter as his fireman. Steve Harris is in the cab of the Ivatt tank No.41249. (*Maurice Cook collection*)

(*above*) Driver Bill May beside a model of Stephenson's Link Motion – this was used to explain an engine's valve motion at mutual improvement classes. Bill spent 46 years on the S&D. (*Bill May collection*)

(*right*) Fireman John Rice surveys the tender of a class 3 freight engine outside Highbridge loco shed in the 1950s. The sand furnace chimney is in the background. (*Terry Fry collection*)

(*above*) Ivatt tank No.41307 with driver George Wheadon, left, and fireman Mike Lewis before taking a goods train to Glastonbury. (*S&DRT collection*)

(*left*) Fireman Terry Fry, left, and driver Les Warren enjoying his pipe on Collett 0-6-0 No.2218 at Highbridge. Who has taken the number plate? (*Terry Fry collection*)

0-6-0 goods No.2881, some time before 1934, at Highbridge loco weighbridge where axle weights were taken. (*Bill May collection*)

3F No.43201 at Highbridge preparing to take out the special train celebrating the centenary of the Somerset Central Railway which opened on 28th August 1854. (*Maurice Cook collection*)

A family affair at Burnham-on-Sea station. Porter Hughie Berryman with his daughter Joan and dog Nipper in 1927. Joan married Fred Fisher, the well-known Templecombe driver. (*Joan Fisher collection*)

(*right*) Percy Jubin, with the station broom, Hughie Berryman and another S&D man stand in front of Burnham signalbox in 1930. The box is now with the S&D Railway Trust at Washford. (*Joan Fisher collection*)

(*below*) A busy goods yard at Bridgwater in the war years. From left to right, foreman Fred Gilbert, Sam Farthing, Gilbert Ashill and Gerry Jennings. (*Dennis Ashill collection*)

Happy children talking to the driver of a holiday special at Burnham-on-Sea on 30th July 1955, the motive power being LMS class 3 No.43248. (*Bill May collection*)

On Easter Monday 1914, a crowded holiday excursion train jumped the rails at Burnham-on-Sea. Fortunately nobody was seriously hurt. The train was hauled by 0-4-4T No.52. (*Keith Barrett collection*)

All the relieved passengers from the 1914 accident at Burnham and, inevitably, local on-lookers pose for a photo of the incident. (*Author's collection*)

3F No.43427 passing Burnham-on-Sea signalbox on a local passenger from Evercreech in August 1959. The small wooden signalbox had four levers and was situated at the end of the platform. Staff who operated the box over the years included Frank Staddon, Arthur Badman and Joseph Lush. (*R.E.Toop*)

A sad occasion for S&D driver Ronald 'Chummy' Andrews as he takes down the Burnham-on-Sea name board. Chummy started on the branch in 1914 and gave 50 years loyal service to the S&D. Except for a short period at Bath, he spent all his railway life on the branch. (*S&DRT collection*)

Index

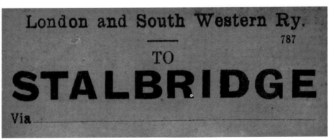